Understanding The Under-Fives

Understanding
The Under-Fives

Donald Baker

Evans

Evans Brothers Limited, London

Published by Evans Brothers Limited,
Montague House,
Russell Square, London WC1

© Donald Baker, 1975

First published 1975

Reprinted 1976

Filmset in 11 on 12 Imprint by
Photoprint Plates Ltd., Rayleigh, Essex
and printed in Great Britain by
T. & A. Constable Ltd., Edinburgh

ISBN 0 237 29134 7   PRA 4899

Contents

This book could not have been written without the advice and help of my wife who has dealt so patiently with my many queries. Neither could it have been written without all those under-fives who have taught me so much about Life.

And a word of appreciation also goes to Clive Carroll for the photographs and to Sheena Pearce for deciphering my original typescript.

Introduction

During the first five years of life, children are learning to live, and learning faster than at any other time in their lives. Moreover, the experiences they have during these years can be as vital as anything else that ever happens to them. Consequently, by the age of five, a child's whole pattern of life may be formed and his future achievements decided. But to many parents—and teachers too—the first five years of a child's life remain a mystery.

For one thing, although we can see a child's body growing, it is not nearly so easy to realise that his thoughts and feelings are also developing, both in depth and direction, just as rapidly. Yet psychologists and biologists alike are generally agreed that the learning process begins in the womb, and that from the day a child is born he understands a great deal more of what is going on around him than adults give him credit for.

Partly because of the natural concern for children's welfare and partly because of the pressure which modern society exerts on all of us to achieve some sort of material success in life, parents, teachers and even the government have now begun to take these first five years very seriously. Quite rightly, we realise that these years are critical and if only we knew how to help a child during this time, we would be giving him a good start in life. But we often fail to understand what is happening in a child's mind or how to deal with his sometimes puzzling behaviour. Giving him the right kind of food to assist his body growth is one thing; providing the right kind of experiences and surroundings that will encourage him to learn about life and living is quite another.

There is a great deal of evidence from psychologists and social workers to support the view that the critically formative years of a child's life are those before he goes to full-time school. And usually, though by no means always, the mother has the major responsibility for what happens to a child during this period.

So in order to help all those who are involved with the education of under-fives to understand some aspects of a pre-school child's behaviour, we shall be looking at the various ways in which young children learn. In particular, we shall be discussing such questions as why a child needs to play and how he goes about playing. We shall then consider how best we can meet his needs by providing emotionally and intellectually stimulating experiences in the home, and lastly we shall refer to the implications which the need for play has for playgroups and nursery schools. In fact, I am suggesting in this book that all the thinking, feeling and doing of an under-five are aspects of play.

Though this book is primarily intended for parents—teachers, especially those concerned with young children, will find the accounts of play techniques helpful in dealing with nursery groups and reception classes, which in some areas already include the 'rising fives'. It will also prove useful to playgroup supervisors and all those mothers who have become involved in playgroup work. The child's world may indeed be a mystery, but unless we try to penetrate and understand some of its secrets, we shall not be able to give a child, who is learning to live during those crucial first five years, the most effective help and patient understanding we can possibly provide.

1 A widening world

In the beginning, the child's world is confined to the walls of his mother's womb, a warm, safe and secret world insulated from the harsh and hostile life outside in one of the most ingenious and efficient suspension systems in existence. Here he lives for the first nine months of his life, totally dependent on his mother for food and any impressions of the world outside he may receive. Though we know very little about his mental processes during this time, it seems fairly safe to assume that his mind is developing just as his body is growing and forming into the baby everyone will admire when he is eventually born.

During the first few months of life, a baby is still completely dependent on his mother. But though she provides his obvious needs such as food and clothing, other less obvious but almost as necessary factors such as security and her body warmth can be overlooked, or if not overlooked, considered to be of little importance.

Nevertheless, a baby does need the reassurance of his mother's arms. He needs the cradling motion which recreates the rhythmic movements he experienced in the comparative safety of the womb. The security which surrounded him then is associated with a new kind of security not totally dependent on his mother. Thus he begins to feel confident in his developing independence. Though in a very limited way he is on his own, his mother is still close, and he can feel the warmth of her body. There is no substitute for a mother's holding and caressing her baby.

Experiments in the United States have indicated that children can even be intellectually retarded if they do not receive this kind of attention from a mother. It was found, for example, that children in institutions who could not identify their source of security with any one adult tended to be under-stimulated and became either apathetic or aggressive, presumably in order to attract adult attention. Under-stimulation in children, who for various reasons have not received close and involved attention from their mothers, sometimes leads to backwardness in speech. The reasons for this are fairly easy to see. If no one has stimulated a response in the child either through caress and gesture, or through 'talk', there is no reaction from the child in terms of either a gurgling chuckle or, later, a few hesitant attempts to imitate sounds. And the babbling stage, as pre-speech is sometimes called, is missed out. In short, a child has not learnt to play with sounds, which is a prerequisite for acquiring language.

Another and very important factor involved in the physical relationship between mother and baby is that of identity. When her baby cries, a mother may pick him up and provide the rhythmic rocking which reassures him. He smiles and she smiles back. So piece by piece he fits each experience into a picture of someone who is very close to him, but yet somehow not actually himself. He is creating a picture of another human being and thus discovering, albeit quite unconsciously, what the human species is like. And in the first instance, of course, a human being is identified with his mother, which makes the mother's role in these early months vitally important. One psychologist has claimed that a child's picture of humanity may depend on what his mother is like. If she satisfies his needs, reassures him with kindness and loving care, he may begin life with confidence. On the other hand, if she is neglectful, giving him little physical security and only increasing his anxieties, he may become frustrated, anxious and uncertain in his own relationships with people later on.

So the baby begins to make contact with a brand-new world through his senses, sight, hearing, touch, taste and smell. He looks up and with eyes gradually learning to focus and follow

2

what he sees he begins to recognise his mother's face. By five months he will almost certainly be responding to her with smiles, human signals of relationship. But sometimes he looks up and sees the enormous head of an adoring aunt or neighbour filling his whole field of vision and strange eyes peering down at him. He screams—and no wonder!

Later in life, when the incident has long been stored away in the memory banks of his subconscious, the face may return in a dream. He has a nightmare in which a face comes nearer and nearer with frightening intensity. We say he should not have eaten so much so late at night but, more probably, the dream recalls the time when an unthinking adult expressed adoration by obliterating the small world the child could see with his limited vision.

So we should always avoid presenting large pictures, big sounds, sudden violent movements, all of which can cause a baby to react in sudden fear and can imprint a memory that is later drawn up from his subconscious and so recreates the original fear.

Following from this, we should never surround a child with too many playthings or confront him with a collection of 'baubles, bangles and beads'. Innumerable dangling and rattling toys can cause over-stimulation with too many sensations for him to cope with adequately. The baby who is still in the cot and pram stage is as yet unable to make a selection from the mass of sense impressions flowing into his consciousness from the world around him. As adults, we have learned to reject the impressions we do not want. For instance, when we are engrossed in a book, we may never hear the ticking of the clock, because by some mental process we can switch off that particular sound stimulus. It is a routine sound to which we are accustomed and which at the moment is not significant. But we may be startled out of our wits if someone taps on the window!

A confusion of sights and sounds can be frightening, so when placing toys in front of a baby's eyes, moderation is the key note.

We frequently forget that, during the first few months of his life, the infant cannot distinguish between sounds of varying importance and significance. He has to learn the rational process of selection. Similarly with the objects he sees, particularly people. As we noticed earlier, by five months, the baby is usually recognising a few familiar faces, but he may respond to the un-

3

familiar with a scream which embarrasses the parents. The cry of fear may be inexplicable to his parents, but for the child it is a very natural reaction to the strange and possibly dangerous. Fear is a very necessary instinct of self-defence in the human and the animal world. It is only when fear becomes obsessional that it loses its defensive use. In a later chapter we shall come back to the question of fear and its function in life.

From the moment a baby is born, then, his world begins to expand and the first five years of his life are crucial in that he has to cope with more information, more experiences and to master more physical and mental tasks than at any other time in his life. Learning to walk and learning to speak are just two of the problems an infant has to solve. Indeed, the way in which a child moves from complete dependence on his mother to an independent life is little short of a miracle—particularly for some children who receive hardly any help or encouragement from parents. So how does it all happen?

Imagine a pebble dropped into a pool. Ripples radiate in widening circles from the point where the stone entered the water. In the same way, a child's exploration of the brand-new world radiates from himself as the centre. At first, nothing else matters, and it is even doubtful whether in the beginning he is aware of people and things that are not actually part of him. After all, he has been attached to his mother for nine months and he now has to learn that he is the centre and source of a life which belongs to him and to no one else.

In other words, during the first two years or so the infant is totally 'egocentric' and refers everything he sees, hears, touches and tastes to himself and to his own point of view. And since he is unable to detach himself mentally from the people and objects around him, he cannot distinguish 'me' from 'not me'. Only gradually does he discover how the world is separated from him. When this happens, we say he is forming 'concepts' and this process has something to do with his acquisition of language.

To illustrate what is meant by egocentricity, we can take a very common example of children's speech. Until he learns differently, a child is the world of total experience and he gives the object he sees a life like his own. 'Naughty chair', he says when he bumps into it. And until he realises that there is a difference between him and the chair, he has no need to use the personal pronoun 'I'. In fact, he progresses through 'Baby wants' to

'Me wants' to 'I want', the final form indicating that he has become conscious of his own existence apart from everything else around him. There are many other implications involved in the notion of egocentricity, especially the recognition of living and non-living things and we shall return to these matters later. In the meantime, we should note that, by the age of five, most of the developments in self-consciousness, and the effects they have on language and thought, have taken place.

Moving into the world

From the age of two or so, the child's world is expanding rapidly, especially as he is now mobile. He can explore situations further afield. No longer is the cot or pram the limit of his world. Now the playpen, the room, the garden and so on become the new boundaries. On his feet he can not only explore things at ground level, but also at arm level. And though from his point of view ransacking drawers, shelves and bookcases may be exploration, parents understandably think otherwise. The difference between 'exploration' and 'ransacking' here is really one of point of view and raises the whole question of 'correct' behaviour and how to go about the business of 'correction'. This is another matter we shall come back to in a later chapter, but it is worth drawing attention to two points regarding what we might consider destructive actions.

Firstly, the child is trying out his newly discovered physical powers to reach, to touch and to move objects. Secondly, the noise made by the falling objects is satisfying in itself. The pleasure lies in 'being a cause', as the psychologists put it. Similar pleasure in destructive play can be observed when piles of bricks other children have built are knocked over. What seems to be happening in these annoying but unavoidable acts is that the two-year-old is demonstrating his newly discovered strength and asserting himself in his small but ever widening world of experience. The falling bricks tell him that he has caused an event to happen. New sensations, new discoveries and, of course, at the same time, new boundaries! How to control the widening circles of his experience by setting new limits which are not purely restrictive is the problem of parental correction, and, as I said, we shall need to discuss it in much more detail.

In probing experiences and making contact with his expanding world, the child involves all his senses, though possibly taste and smell are not so quickly or highly developed at first as sight, sound and touch. On the other hand, we have all noticed how an infant tends to put most things in his mouth. Almost certainly, this is not an exploratory act to find out what the object tastes like, but an extension of the comfort and satisfaction derived from the action of sucking. 'Comforters' survive well into adult life and some people never discard them at all. Finger biting, cigarette and pipe smoking, for example, give satisfaction from the acts of nibbling and suckling, and any soothing effect from nicotine may be quite incidental. A lollipop could serve the same purpose as a pipe, though hardly providing the accepted image of masculinity!

It goes almost without saying that because young children put most things in their mouths, all pills, poisons and potions should be kept well out of their reach. Infants and even older children will start to suck what they can pick up, partly as experiment and partly as a substitute nipple.

The sense of smell seems a late developer, possibly because— unlike other animals which depend on scent for their recognition of other members of their species, for food, and for safety—the human being tends to rely on sight and sound signals.

So as a child moves into a keener awareness that the world consists of objects each having an independent existence, or, as one child psychologist puts it, as he experiences 'the decentring of egocentricity', the detachment of the 'me' from the 'not me', he begins to realise that there are other circles of influence radiating outwards from other people and other things. And as his little bit of 'selfhood' expands into the world, so he begins colliding with them. In simple terms, the opposition he meets may come from hard objects, which do not give way but apparently hit back, or from a more complex form of opposition—for example, parental correction. 'Don't do that!' or a fight over a contested toy or sweet are the uncompromising facts of life. They can also be somewhat frightening.

Consequently, the growing child occasionally retreats into his own world and unconsciously recalls the safety and security associated with his mother. And because mother can no longer carry him around everywhere, he carries something with him which he associates with her. It may be a piece of old clothing (a fragment of an old nightdress is not uncommon) or a tatter of blanket or towel which subconsciously reminds him of his helpless baby days when, as the undisputed centre of the world, his mother cared for his every need.

There is, indeed, no real substitute for the warmth of mother's body experienced through firm, gentle holding, for this is how the baby first identifies the world. If initial experience is not frightening but secure and reassuring, then perhaps later on he will be able to meet his independent life more confidently. But do not be surprised if he wants to keep an object he associates with his babyhood for a while.

A child's latent anxiety is sometimes expressed in rocking movements. Maybe the movement recalls for him the movement he felt when living in his mother's womb, or maybe the repetitive quality of the rocking gives a sense of mastery over some piece of life. It is quite common to see both the clutching of some familiar object and the rocking movements in some children, but only if this behaviour continues well on into childhood—in a six- or seven-year-old for instance—should we begin to ask questions about possible anxieties. Starting school is one of the most anxious moments for a child and might produce 'rocking', and there will certainly be a few examples of it in a playgroup.

What we must always remember is that in the widening area of his experience, a child meets all kinds of opposition, which will modify his own personal behaviour, so that he, like us, eventually integrates with society, first with the family, then with school and ultimately, of course, with the whole world of adult life. In this process, any new encounter might produce temporary anxiety, until it is understood and mentally digested.

We can, perhaps, pursue the image of widening circles a little further. Sometimes, we are concerned because a two- or three-year-old apparently fails to remember what he has been told, or because he takes up one activity only to drop it a few minutes later. Moreover, friends are made and lost almost on a daily basis. Quite often parents are worried by what they mistakenly believe to be their children's lack of 'concentration' and begin to wonder whether their children lack intelligence.

But the reason for this apparent lack of continuity in children's experience is that, on the pattern of our expanding circles, there is no actual connection between each circle, though each one is related to the centre, namely the child. Take the illustration of the pebble again. Every ripple is caused by the pebble, but each one has no visible connection with another. Similarly with a young child's experiences: each one is related to him, but until he reaches the age of three or so, connections, or 'schemas' as psychologists sometimes call them, are not made. In simple language, this means collecting up the bits and pieces of experience that our senses have given us and relating them to each other in a coherent and meaningful pattern, a 'schema', which forms a frame of reference for future experience and exploration. Throughout life we are all constructing new patterns, new schemas, making new relationships between what we see, hear, touch, taste and smell.

Now all these explorations are made through the activity of play, which, for children, is a very serious business indeed. In these days we hear so much about the 'playway' to learning in school, that we may forget that we all learn through play from the very beginning. It all depends on what we mean by 'play'. To help us appreciate what is happening to a child as he develops mentally, emotionally and physically and how he experiences the process of growing away from mother-dependence into the world of total independence, we shall look at the nature of play and the various forms it takes, together with methods and means of stimulating it and then try to understand some of its more puzzling aspects.

There is no doubt at all that unless children play, they are not only denied the fundamental means of learning, but also create for themselves and for society many problems of behaviour which society itself has later to try to solve. Why is it, for example, that most people do not go around smashing up the furniture or knocking other people over the head? And why is it that some people do?

Part of the answer may lie in the quality of play a child experiences during the first five years of life. And so it becomes imperative that we understand what children are doing and why, and more important still, how we can encourage their play.

Before moving on to discuss play itself, one point cannot be overstressed. In everything we do with and for children, we must take what they say and do seriously. Condescension in language and attitude is disrespectful to children's intelligence and trust, and if we do not respect them, or if we fail to be as courteous to them as we are to adults, we should not be surprised when their behaviour sometimes makes us describe them as 'little horrors' or worse. The key to understanding a child's awkward behaviour frequently lies in the behaviour of his parents. The responsibility of all adults who come into contact with children, especially the under-fives, is very great indeed. To underline the importance of our attitude towards children, I cannot do better than to quote a few words from Gabriel Marcel, a French philosopher, who writes: 'Think of a small child who brings you three bedraggled dandelions it has picked by the wayside; it expects you to admire them, it awaits from you a recognition of the value of its gift; and if you lose it, or put it down carelessly, or do not stop talking to express your delight, you are guilty of a sin against love'. In the child's world, it is better if he meets love expressed in care, consideration, courtesy and encouragement, than if he meets with rejection or is ignored. In the next chapter, we shall see how best we can enter imaginatively into the child's world of play.

2   The concept of play

Play is not something we do when work is over. Adults may think that play is a leisure activity, but for children, work and play can be the same thing. One four-year-old whose father was a builder remarked as he pretended to paint the climbing frame: 'I'm playing at work!' And I can distinctly remember 'cementing' cracks in the garden path with mud. It took a whole morning, as, armed with trowel and a great deal of concentration, I plugged those cracks, and, incidentally, learnt that mud is no substitute for cement. In 'playing at work', we also learn!

We have only to watch children on the beach carrying innumerable buckets of sand and water from one place to another, or tunnelling furiously through mountains resembling miniature Mont Blancs, to realise how hard children do 'work' at their play. In years to come, children will discover that there is a regulation somewhere that lays down how many buckets are to be carried and emptied in an hour. And so, as Wordsworth put it, 'Shades of the prison house begin to close about the growing boy . . .' But the under-fives can play at work all day without getting bored. So we must try to prevent that prison closing in too soon and too quickly. And the most important thing for parents and teachers to know is what children's play is all about, so that work can still be play for a little longer.

The necessity for play

Play is absolutely serious and utterly necessary and it must be treated as such, whether we are discussing the play of children or of adults. And we all play at something. For example, the week-end sailor, who takes out his dinghy on a lake or in the shelter of a cliff-edged bay, may secretly imagine that he is crossing the Atlantic or discovering New Zealand. Not that he would admit it, for adults are a little self-conscious about their own playing, which is one of the reasons why it is sometimes difficult for them to accept children's play seriously.

Indeed, the man in his sailing dinghy is an example of adult fantasy play and fantasy play serves a most important function in life. Without fantasy we might all suffer some sort of emotional collapse. Part of the function of fantasy play is to learn how to cope with fear, a fundamental emotion which can cause all kinds of mental havoc if it is not allowed to develop as a normal human response to the unfamiliar. We shall discuss fantasy play in more detail in the next chapter, but two points about it must be stressed here.

Firstly, fantasy and reality are sometimes closely interwoven in children's play. At other times, children realise their playing is pretence and will say 'It's only a game'. It needs experience and a great deal of sensitivity on the part of parents and teachers to recognise play which is 'for real' and play which is 'only pretending'.

Secondly, children are frequently upset because we dismiss as pretence what is to them absolutely real. On the other hand, they sometimes consider an adult crazy when he tries to humour a child by pretending to believe in his fantasy. For the adult, the child's shifting worlds of fantasy and reality are extremely difficult to pin down. One thing we must never do is to tell a child that his fantasy is a lie, for the under-five who claims to have seen three lions in the garden *has* seen them in his fantasy garden—and by seeing them may have overcome, to some extent, a latent fear of lions and monsters and 'things that go bump in the night'.

Children's play, then, is serious and must be treated seriously. It is also vitally necessary to them, since without opportunities

11

to play children will be severely restricted, sometimes permanently, in their intellectual and emotional life. At the same time, children's play is fun and totally absorbing.

Play, however, is not only necessary to the development of thought and feeling, but also essential to physical growth in terms of a child's increasing awareness of his bodily functions. Through play, a child reaches out into the widening world of intellect, emotion and physical space.

Play is a form of exploration of oneself and of one's world. A child discovers he has a voice by crying. Soon he realises that when he cries he gets attention, and so he begins to learn that sound communicates with the world outside him. And, as we saw earlier, he first communicates with his mother. Later his babbling baby-talk forms itself into collections of sounds we call words and to his parents' great delight he may say 'mama' and 'dada'. Eventually, he begins to talk and to put words together into sentences. He can now express his needs verbally in more detail and is able to contact the world outside him through meaningful sounds which other people, not necessarily his mother, understand. So he acquires language.

But a child also has to find out how much physical space he takes up, and he does this by crawling over and under the furniture, testing dimensions and distances against the size of his own body. Some never learn this properly and people say they are clumsy, because they continually bump into things. One explanation may be that their parents were over-protective in the early months of their childhood, and consequently denied them opportunities for exploratory physical play by keeping them in a cot or playpen far longer than necessary. But, of course, unless we have exceptional memories, we shall have long since forgotten that our parents prevented us from taking reasonable risks. And there are some risks that children really do have to take, even if climbing a tree does seem a perilous business to naturally anxious parents!

Play as risk

As a child becomes more mobile and his manipulative skill increases, he tests his strength by hitting and hammering, climbing, running and jumping. Again, there may be risks involved in some of these activities, but we have to remember that over-protection

A two-year-old explores physical space

can cause a child to lack confidence in his own abilities and because he is never allowed to try them out he becomes at best clumsy and at worst accident-prone.

A brief word about the meaning of 'accident-prone' might be helpful. Being prone to accidents is not an inherited characteristic. The phrase is really a popular description of a common phenomenon in which simple clumsiness like dropping plates may turn into something more serious like putting one's own or other people's lives in danger. The reason for being accident-prone is essentially a failure to coordinate mind and body. In other words, the body does not respond to the mind's instructions quickly or precisely enough. Effective coordination can only develop out of many experiences of responding to various stimuli until these responses become virtually instinctive and instantaneous. For example, when we learn to drive a car, we first of all consciously decide to brake, change gear and so on. After further experience, these conscious actions become almost automatic and immediate. The more we consciously *think* about what we are doing, the slower our response becomes and the less positive our actions. We lack confidence in our ability to carry out various physical tasks.

A child, therefore, should be given plenty of opportunities to explore his physical powers in climbing and balancing, crawling and running so that he learns not only how to control these powers and use them effectively, but also how to relate his own body space to the space and distances he meets in his environment. Thus he learns how to make judgements with confidence.

Moreover, if he lacks confidence in exercising his body's powers, not only is he more likely to be prone to physical accidents but he may also appear emotionally timid, withdrawn and over-dependent on adults in general and his mother in particular. As we shall see in later chapters, there are various ways in which play helps children—and adults for that matter—to come to terms with their fears. Playing at events which are frightening in order to *play out* the fear of them is a common function of play. For example, a child will play at visiting the dentist or hospital and by so doing he is gradually accepting his fear and dealing with it. Stories can have the same effect and we shall return to these points later.

Intellectually, a child who has been restricted in his play activities may find mastering new methods and acquiring new knowledge, even learning to read, a frightening business, and he may even develop a kind of 'mental blockage' which is only a result of his latent anxiety. Sometimes, because the situation presents so many new experiences, a fear of school develops. In some cases, not always obvious to parents, the fear grows to such proportions that the child finds ways of evading school. Stomach aches, skin rashes, bilious turns may appear as symptoms of his anxiety. Obviously, these are extreme cases, but they are, nevertheless, quite common and their causes may lie in parental over-protection from risk which most forms of play must inevitably involve.

Play as exploration

In the first instance, then, the essence of play is trying something out, or, to put it another way, play is partly improvisation. By a process of trial and error, a child discovers that some speech and certain actions produce satisfying results and some do not.

Eventually, by repeating sounds and movements which are both satisfying to himself and also acceptable to other people in that they respond to his needs, he establishes behaviour patterns. So he learns to speak and to move in his own little social circle, first in the home, then in the world at large.

At the same time, he is learning to cope with fear and anxiety and all the problems, both large and small, that life inevitably presents to him. And we should never underestimate the emotional upheaval and the wrench in relationships that occur when a five-year-old first goes to school. His world is no longer a room in a house with familiar figures of father and mother, brothers and sisters, but may be a space bigger than he has ever seen before and filled with more children than he has ever met. The great strength of playgroups for under-fives lies in their potential for effecting a gradual weaning away from mother attachment to independence, which is a valuable contribution to the emotional and social development of the young child. But, of course, attendance at playgroups is not always possible for various reasons, and this makes it all the more necessary for parents to realise some of the stresses and strains put on the under-five, who has to face just as real and just as enormous problems as confront adults in their world.

Play as order

So far we have suggested that play is a process of discovery and exploration of the body, mind and feelings. Play, however, is not only a means of exploring oneself and one's environment, but is also an attempt to create order out of what must appear a chaotic mass of impressions to the child.

One interesting phenomenon which illustrates this point is that a child who comes from a home where there is little or no order or routine, where things are left lying about all over the place and where meals do not appear at regular times, will often spend long play sequences 'tidying up'. I remember watching a four-year-old girl in a playgroup constantly folding and refolding her doll's clothes, neatly putting away the ironing board and emptying and repacking her shopping basket. Plainly, she was trying to establish order in her own world of play over which she had control. All her activities were compensations for lack of order in her real home. On the other hand, a child from an over-

Learning to control physical movements.

tidy home will compensate in the opposite way and try to create some disorder. In the latter case, just getting hands covered in paint during finger-painting sessions helps to do this in a controlled and productive situation. Obviously, there should be a happy medium struck between tidiness and disorder, routine and flexibility.

To some extent, order depends on the predictable quality of events: if we do something, then the result will be so and so. We learn that we get burnt if we put our finger in the fire. This is certain and predictable; it will always happen like that.

But we also learn to give meaning and shape to our actions by discovering that certain sounds and certain actions, signals like smiling for example, produce predictable results. So a particular inflexion of the voice requires an answer; another inflexion does not, and in this way we learn the difference between question and answer.

A need for security and order, depending on the predictable quality of events, lies behind a child's rhythmic stamping by which he seems to learn that in controlling the movements of his feet he can make a predictable noise. Spoon banging, table tapping—not confined to children by any means—jumping and hopping are similar activities and rely for their effect on the discovery of body rhythms, which, in their turn, depend on the natural rhythms of the body's function, the heartbeat, breathing and so on. In fact, the simplest rhythm that a young child responds to in music is the steady beat which reproduces the rhythm of the heart, for this must be one of the first sensations of which a baby is conscious. In the first place, of course, it will be his mother's heartbeat and then, subconsciously, his own. I say 'subconsciously', though it is during the first five years that a child becomes aware of such physical factors as heartbeat and breathing. As one four-year-old remarked after doing some strenuous work/play: 'Stop thumping heart!' It was pointed out that it would be unfortunate for him if it did!

Although mastery of movements, emotions and ideas is encouraged through the use of physical rhythms like stamping and hopping, clapping and jumping, or just making repetitive sounds with his voice or repeating a new word over and over again, security and order are further reinforced by playing out events children have witnessed. So they repeat, either actually or imaginatively, the relationships between father and mother, occupations of parents or perhaps just 'playing house'. In these activities, children are accepting patterns of life and behaviour within their own schemes of things, and we shall need to say more about this kind of play in a later chapter.

Some parents hope to push their child on more quickly by emphasising intellectual development. Perhaps they teach their child to read and possibly allow him to watch adult T.V. programmes including the news. The news, however, is really not suitable for any under-fives to watch, especially scenes of violence and destruction. A four-year-old will have considerable difficulty in distinguishing between what is 'real' or just a 'story' and consequently could suffer some emotional disturbance by watching war scenes and similar sequences. This question of truth and fiction brings us back to the point about fantasy and reality referred to earlier. Though we shall return to this question in the next chapter, it is worth remembering that young children cannot distinguish between what is reality and what is pretence and part of the function of play is to help them to make this

Playing house under the table.

distinction.

It frequently happens that older parents, though over-protecting their child from the risks of play, unthinkingly expose him to the greater risks of the real world presented on the T.V. screen and this can adversely affect a child's emotional development. The parents may be far more concerned with intellectual progress, and by emphasising this in terms of teaching a child to read and treating him as an adult capable of making the necessary adult responses to what he sees, often end up doing more harm than good.

I remember one four-year-old, who could read fluently and carry on apparently intelligent, adult conversations, 'reverting' to boisterous, almost uncontrolled physical activities. He was, of course, only going through those phases of emotional and physical play that he had not experienced. There are no short cuts to adulthood, despite what parents may think. It is better for children to play at their own pace than to be pushed into experiences they are not yet ready for.

18

The psychology of play

At this point it might be useful to give a simple account of the psychology of play. The psychological explanation of play is, unfortunately, a very complex business and no two psychologists are really agreed on its precise function, though most accept that it serves two general purposes.

Firstly, it is a means of exploring physical, emotional and intellectual experiences and, secondly, it enables us to assimilate these experiences into behaviour patterns, social conventions and frames of reference against which we can test future explorations of experience.

In practical terms, the process seems to work something like this. Play is first an improvisation, a process of trial and error, almost literally to see 'what happens if', or what results when we do or say something. In the second place, it is a kind of repetition or rehearsal of those improvisations, so that we build structures of thought, speech and action. And this latter process in play involves the use of rules, a form of ritual or repetition of words and movements which explains, perhaps, the rhythmic stampings and the repeating of familiar sounds and words. There is security in knowing what happens next in rhythm, sound or story, and this may be the reason why children love to hear familiar stories repeated always in exactly the same way.

The whole process of play is stated so concisely by Desmond Morris (who admittedly writes from a biologist's point of view) that it is worth quoting his description of play and how it works:

1. You shall investigate the unfamiliar until it has become familiar.
2. You shall impose rhythmic repetition on the familiar.
3. You shall vary this repetition in as many ways as possible.
4. You shall select the most satisfying of these variations and develop these at the expense of others.
5. You shall combine and re-combine these variations with one another.
6. You shall do all this for its own sake, as an end itself.

The last point should answer those parents and teachers who adversely criticise 'play', either in playgroups, first schools or even in the home, because it appears aimless and disorganised and produces no measurable results.

Though Desmond Morris's description of play is comprehensive and accurate, it leaves out the importance of play as a means of co-operation with others. Most of his points are concerned, at least by implication, with the individual, but play also involves other children and other people.

Earlier, I suggested that the physical aspect of play was to help children discover 'body awareness', the amount of space their bodies physically occupy. If we regard a child's development in terms of ever-widening concentric circles of discovery radiating from himself as the centre of everything, then as he gradually moves outwards from this centre he inevitably meets other children who are doing the same thing. His circles of awareness overlap with circles of awareness belonging to other people. Sometimes there will be clashes of interest, sometimes common interests, and it is in these areas of overlapping that friendships are made and broken. We can call what happens in these areas 'group play' and all children should have some opportunity for it, either in a playgroup or, if this is not possible, by inviting other children into the home to play. This is especially necessary for an only child, simply because, just as there is clumsy behaviour in those who have not learned body awareness, so there are clumsy relationships among those who have not learned 'mental awareness'.

There is, I believe, a mental space which people take up just as they occupy physical space, and we have to learn how much space our egoism occupies. In play, children can learn how to modify their mental attitudes so that they can come to terms with others. Spatial and mental awareness can be encouraged in group or co-operative play.

If we analyse individual play a little further, we can use a description which Peter Slade gave many years ago, but which is still valid and useful. Certainly these descriptions can help us provide situations for play and play materials.

Peter Slade suggests two forms of play: 'personal' and 'projected'. In 'personal play', the distinction between fantasy and reality almost, if not actually, disappears. It is a world that the child creates for himself, within which, because it is ordered as the child wants it to be, life is lived often as a reflection of the adult world. So we see children playing fathers, mothers, monsters, pirates, cats, ladybirds and snakes. In fact, in 'personal play', a child is using his whole body, a point that corroborates the claim of the great Swiss psychologist, Jean Piaget, that children learn through actual movement, or *sensori-motor perception*. This means that a child actually *becomes* a thing or a person. He may be a motor car one minute and the driver the next. In each case, he is learning by doing, and eventually he will be able to think about the thing or person without having physically to play it out. By actually being or playing the thing he is forming a concept of it.

In 'projected play' treasures are used first and later, toys. In this form of play, the child projects his consciousness onto or into an object, a piece of wood, a box or a teddy bear, and he obviously imagines that the object has a life of its own. 'Projected play', as Peter Slade points out, is characterised by the stillness of the child. There is usually little actual bodily movement, except for the hands which are used to manipulate the object, literally to 'play *with* it'. Important in the encouragement of 'projected play' are toys which, however, need to be discussed separately, since choosing the right kind of toys for children is a vital factor in children's development. In the main, toys should allow for a child's imagination to create new uses for the toy, so that it can become *any* thing. The more representative of actuality a toy is, the sooner will boredom arise, simply because the opportunities for trial and error of mind and body are thwarted by the limitations of the specific object.

Most children will combine 'personal' and 'projected' play, the play sequences becoming more complicated as the child's imagination develops. But we usually notice a three-year-old playing almost entirely on his own, projecting himself into objects, toys and imaginary people. He talks to himself very often, an activity in which he is playing with words and sounds and gaining fluency in speech. Though he may show an interest in other children, he is much more likely to play on his own and not want to co-operate with any other children in their playing.

By the age of four, however, a child is usually moving away from himself, extending those circles of awareness we have referred to, and he is then ready for group playing. The point of making these comments is that we should not worry if a child seems solitary until he reaches the age of three or so. This is quite natural, because he is still in the egocentric state of development and relates the whole world to himself. As he becomes aware of himself as having a distinct and separate life from the things and people around him, he is also conscious of the need to play with them. Thus, from depending on one or very few people, his mother and father for instance, he gradually comes to need more and more people, not necessarily those belonging to his own family.

A further factor relating to the child's growing awareness of himself as distinct from his environment is the distinction he begins to make between fantasy and reality. This has many implications for life as a whole and we shall go on to discuss this matter in detail. Before doing so, perhaps it will help to summarise the function of play and the reasons why it is so important that parents and teachers understand it.

We can say that play is serious, absorbing, necessary, that it is the means by which a child explores his own physical, emotional and intellectual capabilities. Play is also a means of discovering the qualities in other people and other things. Putting these two functions together, play enables a child to experience the world piece by piece and to adjust his own ego, his selfhood, to the pattern of his environment as it unfolds before him. In this way, he learns the social conventions of speech and behaviour. Children begin to 'create roles' for themselves, that is to say, they begin to shape their individual personalities, partly from what they inherit and partly from contact with the world around them. Plainly, it is of the utmost importance that we realise what is happening in children's play during those first five years and it is obviously necessary that we provide children with stimulating play situations, which encourage their personal and social development. For the development of personality is what play is all about; to deny it in some way is to deny an essential characteristic of our humanity. Or, as Peter Slade puts it so aptly when referring to personal and projected play: 'These two early types of play have an important bearing on the building of Man, his whole behaviour, and his ability to fit in with society. Play opportunity, therefore, means gain and development'.

We shall now go on to look at some of the ways in which these opportunities for play can be given.

3 Fantasy play

In this chapter, we shall pursue the meaning of play a little further by looking at a particular aspect of it, and, though this chapter is headed 'fantasy play', in a sense *all* play is fantasy, which is one of the reasons why parents are sometimes puzzled by their children's activities. This is especially true of such common phenomena as 'lying' and 'the imaginary friend', which often cause parents concern. In this chapter we shall be discussing these common but curious aspects of behaviour. We shall also be discussing the psychological function of fantasy in the emotional and intellectual development of children.

There is no doubt that many parents are distressed by the fantasy worlds in which their children seem to live, and the distress is shared by some teachers. 'They're making it all up!' or 'They're telling lies!' are all too frequent comments. But there is a very great difference between fantasy in play and telling lies.

A lie is deliberate and self-conscious, a fabrication constructed with a specific purpose in mind, such as avoiding punishment or compensating for a feeling of guilt or inadequacy. But play itself, as we discussed in the last chapter, is very often an unconscious activity and, to quote Desmond Morris again, 'for its own sake . . . an end in itself'. Lying is usually deliberate and conscious; play is frequently spontaneous and without apparent purpose.

Lying, then, is a deliberate and conscious evasion of an awkward or distressing situation; play on the other hand, is not an evasion but a process of acceptance. Lying is usually for other people's benefit, whereas play is for oneself. It is difficult, though I imagine not utterly impossible, to deceive oneself. In fact, self-deception, in which fantasy play becomes a lived-out lie, is characteristic of the mental illness in which the patient withdraws completely from the real world to live in his own fantasy world leading him into all kinds of nightmarish horrors or happy euphoria. Quite simply, the fantasy world is a means of self-defence, an uncontrolled escape route from the problems and anxieties with which the patient has been unable to cope. There are many and varied reasons given for this particular kind of withdrawal, but I have a suspicion that it can arise, just as uncontrolled, irrational violence can arise, from lack of play opportunities in early life.

What most of us learn as we grow older is that the world of fantasy, where we can manipulate events and people as we wish, is a different and separate world from the one in which we actually live. If we continually fail to distinguish these worlds in later life, we may begin to believe that the fantasy is real. For instance, if we have not learned through play the quality of our own strength and that fighting can really hurt, we might do actual harm to someone. Perhaps, though I have no concrete evidence of this, the violence that erupts on our streets is partly due to a failure to play early in life, or a denial of the opportunity for indulging in fantasy during the first five years of life. Quite a number of people live in 'Walter Mitty' style worlds. Because they never had sufficient opportunities for play when they were children they have been unable to discover their potentials and their limitations. Not knowing the reach and range of their physical, emotional and intellectual abilities, they imagine these abilities are greater than they actually are and fantasy is confused with reality.

On the other hand, if we have learned to distinguish fantasy from reality, fantasy, either in individual play or in various art forms, can provide a *valuable* escape route from a reality that inevitably becomes too much for most of us sometimes. Both

24

Fighting play.

play and art, which are in some respects the same thing, can serve this purpose.

It is not very fashionable in these days to talk about art as an escape. It is usually said that we must forever be confronted by the social reality of poverty, violence, famine, flood, fire and 'the heart-ache and the thousand natural shocks that flesh is heir to . . .' But those who advocate social realism in art and play forget the uncomfortable fact that without some form of recreation, which is really the re-creation of sanity and order in minds distressed by events that seem too difficult to handle, we shall probably suffer an anxiety neurosis.

This kind of escape for many older people lies in radio and T.V. serials. They follow with avid interest the fictitious lives of the characters, living them out as if they were real. Most people know that they are not, but underlying this attitude towards stories and plays is the feeling that the whole world of the Archers or the Forsytes is safely and securely ordered by someone who knows the overall pattern. The author is a kind of god, who keeps us safe and secure in his fantasy world, just as a good mother, father or teacher will surround their children with reassurance and safety in their worlds of individual play.

Fantasy as therapy

There is no doubt that fantasy in play is fundamental to learning about ourselves and about our world, but it also serves other important purposes, which, though not quite so obvious, are just as essential. For fantasy is 'therapeutic'—it 'does us good'.

The reasons for this are twofold. In the first place, fantasy play enables us to cope with and sometimes even to master our fears and all those problems and questions which we continually meet in life. And just as adults need to escape into their own version of a dream world where they know there will be a happy ending, so children need opportunities for similar 'escapes', though 'escape' is hardly the right word to describe a very necessary function of fantasy play. J. R. R. Tolkien, whose tales about the Hobbits became classics in his own lifetime, more accurately calls fantasy a means of 'consolation', because there is, he says, 'the joy of the happy ending'. And it seems to me that all of us, children and adults alike, need this consolation of joy to help

Substitution therapy: in hitting the picture of the dragon the child may be quelling his own fear of monsters.

us cope with the fret and worry of daily life.

For example, a child who is frightened by imaginary monsters may find consolation in being told a story in which an imaginary child successfully deals with monsters. Indirectly, he identifies with the child in the story, but the story, which is really a form of play, protects him from actually experiencing the terror. Maurice Sendak's delightful story, *Where the Wild Things Are*, illustrates this point and we shall come back to this in the chapter on 'story play'.

In the second place, fantasy is therapeutic because it helps us to deal with our guilt, which, in its own peculiar way, can cause anxieties of all kinds. For children, guilt often arises on account of the displeasure they believe they have caused an adult, or because they vaguely recognise they have offended some social code. The cause might be as simple as breaking mother's teacup, spilling the milk, wetting the bed or a host of frequently minor accidents which the sensitive parent will deal with sympathetically, but which the child may magnify out of all proportion.

27

In fantasy play, guilt can be dissolved by the ancient device of the 'scapegoat'. Usually for a child this will be 'Teddy' or a favourite doll. When play involves 'Teddy' getting a spanking, 'Teddy' is really the child's scapegoat and 'naughty Teddy' actually means 'naughty me', but by a process of mental substitution, the child manages to avoid parental displeasure. Adults have their scapegoats too, and whenever the villain in a story gets his just deserts, we may be subconsciously identifying ourselves with him.

The theory of fantasy as therapy is one mainly associated with the psychologist Sigmund Freud who developed it in connection with mentally disturbed patients, but, in general, his work has now been given a much wider application. Its importance in the life of under-fives cannot be overestimated, because the therapeutic functions of fantasy play arise from the protection it seems to offer against the frightening, the unpleasant and the mischievous. In the chapter on story play, we shall be looking at particular ways in which therapy can take place in storytelling, but at the moment we shall try to see how fantasy play actually works.

The functions of fantasy

Firstly, it is quite possible to prepare children for unpleasant and potentially frightening experiences by playing them out *before* they actually happen. For instance, injections of some kind are common these days, but never pleasant. I have myself played at being doctors and nurses with children and we have given 'injections' to each other. And though I hate having injections myself, I always *pretend* to enjoy the experience, at the same time explaining why we have to have 'the needle', as children often call it. I believe this kind of fantasy play therapy can help children deal with the real thing if and when it comes.

Secondly, children play *at* their fears until they have either played them *out* or at least come to terms with them. Many things, unknown or undreamed of by adults, can frighten children. Monsters and nameless dreads existing on staircases or in dark corners are very real to children and we should take these seriously and not dismiss them as silly. Otherwise we will only drive the fears further in, because the child will be embarrassed to talk about them.

In a moment we shall be discussing the nature of fantasy play in detail, but we can note here that *all* play is imitative, or, as sociologists call it, a form of 'role-playing'. I mention this because it seems clear that children often assume the role of aggressor in the fantasy play which arises from an attempt to deal with fear. For example, children who are frightened by pictures of monsters they have seen on T.V. will pretend to be monsters themselves and frighten other children. Or, since ghosts (where do children get the idea of ghosts from in the first place?) frighten them, they play at ghosts and scare each other almost to the point of hysterical terror.

It is difficult, if not impossible, to explain exactly how the process of playing at frightening things can help us overcome our fear of them. Freud's daughter, Anna, suggested that by becoming the aggressor or the 'frightener', we somehow put up a defence against fear and at the same time are protected from anxiety about it.

One of the earliest child psychologists, Melanie Klein, whose approach to the psychology of childhood has had a tremendous though often unacknowledged influence on the education of the very young, claimed that in play we are unconsciously expressing our fears, conflicts, pleasures and hates. But however play is explained, it seems to work, and we should never overlook the therapeutic value of fantasy in play, because there is no doubt that it is a means of dealing with emotions like fear and anger. At least we can appreciate what is happening in this aspect of children's play, even if we do not understand exactly *how* it works.

Now all this may seem to lead us a long way from the meaning of fantasy in play for the under-fives, but I firmly believe that the play of children and their future life as adults are of a piece. And in any case, the element of fantasy in play is an important and vital function of play both for children and for adults. For fantasy underlines the fundamental need in everyone of us to escape temporarily into a world where everything is all right, either because we have learned to make it so in our personal world of play when we were children, or because someone else has presented this world to us in art forms like novels and plays. The 'happy ending' in a story or play may indicate an escape from reality because events never happen quite like that, but it also shows how much we all need some kind of security in life, and we seek it in familiar routines and predictable conclusions where events are ordered just as they should be. The ritual of the story-telling confirms us in the feeling—it is hardly rational—that ultimately all shall be well.

To summarise at this point and incidentally to confirm J. R. Tolkien's belief in the power of fantasy to create 'joy', I can do no better than quote an American sociologist, Peter Berger, who writes: '. . . one of the most pervasive features of play is that it is usually a joyful activity . . . It is this curious quality, which belongs to all joyful play, that explains the liberation and peace such play provides'. And there was joy, liberation and peace in the four-year-old girl, referred to in the previous chapter, who continually tidied up because she came from a disorganised home. It was her attempt to restore some sort of order to her own world, and she did it in fantasy over which she had complete control.

Maybe this example does suggest an escape from reality, but at least she was liberated from the disorder which offended her, and in her play experienced joy and peace, if only temporarily, though I personally doubt whether a four-year-old ever com-pletely separates life and play. And this leads us to consider the nature of fantasy in more detail.

It often seems as if fantasy and reality are indistinguishable to the very young child, and, indeed, much of a child's play is not *like* life, it *is* life. As I said earlier, all play is a form of fantasy and it is better to discuss 'fantasy *in* play' than 'fantasy play', as if it were quite different from other types of play.

The psychology of fantasy

It is the air of unreality in play that can lead adults to distrust the whole concept of play as part of any education system, whatever the age of the child. In order to see how fantasy in play is not only valuable but necessary to a child's personal development we shall look at two aspects of fantasy which have been described by Susanna Millar in an excellent book *The Psychology of Play* : 'It [fantasy] moves from fragmentary, disjointed bits of pretence to integrated and internally consistent sequences of make-believe.' Although we could split hairs over definitions, I think it is feasible to consider 'pretence' and 'make-believe' as more or less the same thing.

In the first place, the 'disjointed bits of pretence' are simply imitations of what a child has seen or heard. They have no connection with each other, but are merely imitative, or to use the technical term, 'mimetic'. Some examples will illustrate what is meant by unconnected imitations or 'mimings'.

At one moment a three-year-old girl may stand with arms akimbo or arms folded in exact imitation of the way her mother stands. The next moment, she is barking like a dog. The shift from miming what she has seen her mother doing to imitating the noise she has heard a dog make has no connection at all, and the adult finds it difficult to follow the imaginative leaps from one piece of imitation to another.

On the other hand, it sometimes appears as if it is not so much a question of making leaps from one piece of imitation to another, but rather of superimposing imitations on each other. A three-year-old boy will race round the room making quite reasonable imitations of a car engine and changing gears. Is he the driver or the car? Because he has not yet learned to distinguish people from things and is still to some extent in that egocentric stage mentioned earlier, he is very likely both *person* and *thing* at the same time. If we ask him to tell us who or what he is at any one moment, he will almost certainly find it impossible to answer. In fact, the questions are really meaningless to him because he still feels that the whole world is part of him and he can not yet distinguish clearly between fantasy and reality. As Piaget puts it very neatly: 'The child . . . [tends] to confuse . . . the psychical and physical'.

Another aspect of 'disjointed bits of pretence' relates to the way a child acquires language. For instance, children will read a paper or a book holding it like their fathers or mothers do, but instead of actually reading it, which, of course, they are not able to do, they talk gibberish, pretending to read, though it may be that a great deal of adult speech does sound like gibberish to a child.

At first, fragments of sound are repeated in the 'babbling' stage we referred to in the last chapter, and then a word, often any word, is said over and over again. I can distinctly remember being fascinated by the word 'government', the meaning of which I had no idea, but it must have been a word that made some sort of impact on my senses from hearing it on the radio.

Sometimes the word a child repeats will be recognisable, at other times it will not. And usually in this fragmented stage of imitation, a word will be repeated quite out of its context. A three-year-old boy on a bus repeated 'swanky one' whatever his mother said to him, no doubt because the word 'swanky' attracted him by its sound if not its sense. In fact, it is the sound of a word which seems to appeal to a child long before its actual meaning is understood, and by repeating that sound he is able to explore its quality in similar-sounding meaningless words. 'Hello uncle!' may become 'uncle, wuncle, nuncle, buncle, puncle' and so on. The basic sound is varied by changing the initial consonant, especially in what are called 'labials', that is, the sounds 'p', 'b' and 'w'. The reason for this particular variation may be that such labial sounds are a natural development from the so-called 'babbling stage' of one- or two-year-olds. But by the age of four or five, a child will usually have separated jumbles of isolated sounds into meaningful patterns of speech and will be able to carry on a fairly intelligent conversation. Indeed, unless there are any emotional or physical factors preventing it, by the age of five or so, a child will have mastered all the basic sentence structures of his native tongue.

I have been stressing the characteristic chanting of words and sounds by two- and three-year-olds, or the way in which they repeat words without being aware of their meaning, because some parents often mistakenly believe thay have taught their child to say very difficult words, which they then ask him to recite in front of adoring visitors. Any child will try to repeat parrot fashion a word or sound without having the slightest idea of its meaning. Two simple examples, one using a word and one using numbers, will show what I mean and should underline my earlier point that there are no short cuts to learning to speak, count, read or to life itself.

Talking to a three-year-old about Eric Thompson's *Magic Roundabout*, the storyteller was asked: 'Will they say "mollusc"?' Obviously, the three-year-old had watched the T.V. programme and found the sound of it attractive. When he was told that the word would come in the story, the child said 'Isn't "mollusc" a funny word?' And, incidentally, the great strength of Eric Thompson's dialogue in *The Magic Roundabout* lies in the use of words which children can pronounce and find funny, though they may have little idea of their meaning.

Another example will show that even a five-year-old has not always grasped the meaning, or, as psychologists would say, the 'concept' of numbers, except to realise that one number is bigger than another. The following dialogue took place with five-year-olds.

> *Adult :* Do you have dinner at school?
> *First child :* I go home three times.
> *Second child* (not to be outdone): I go home to dinner ten times!

Apart from knowing that ten is greater than three, the second child had no understanding of the *meaning* of ten.

Having spent some time looking at the fragments of imitation in a child's use of words and sounds, we must go on to discuss another important aspect of fantasy in 'disjointed bits of pretence'. This can be seen in the 'projected play' which involves a child playing with objects.

A three-year-old will use things as toys on which he projects isolated bits of his experience. In this way, he is trying out the pieces of information he is constantly receiving from the outside world through his senses. We often see children playing with dolls and teddy bears which are rocked, scolded, fed and sometimes roughly handled. By playing with objects or toys in this way, the child eventually graduates to playing without them. In other words, he is learning to handle his thought, the concepts we mentioned earlier, and eventually he is able to imagine speech and actions without actually having the people or the objects in front of him.

In the first place, then, fantasy or make-believe is a collection of fragmentary experiences expressed in isolated, 'disjointed bits of pretence' without much obvious connection between them. The imitations, and they often are merely imitations or 'mimickings', of speech and action, may have no actual meaning for the child at all at this stage of his development, despite what parents may claim for their offspring.

By the age of five or so, most children will be fitting these fragments of imitation into meaningful patterns. For example, they can say sentences, the previously separate sounds and words now being arranged in order. In the same way, the five-year-old has also learnt the simple conventions of family and social life. He is beginning to understand the limits of his ego, and therefore what he can do and what society, rightly or wrongly, will not allow him to do. His physical, emotional and intellectual reach and range are being defined. Often he will resent this obvious restriction on his attitudes and behaviour and this is where opportunities in the second stage of fantasy in play can be a great help in preparing him for the world of full-time school.

In the second phase, fantasy in play, to repeat Susanna Millar's phrase, consists of 'internally consistent sequences of make-believe'. This may sound a little complicated, but it is really quite simple to understand. All that is being said is that 'the disjointed bits of pretence' are now put together into a narrative. Instead of merely banging a spoon on the table because it makes a predictable sound, the child will use the spoon to stir a pudding, which is part of a meal, which is then eaten by friends, who may be dolls and teddies or who may be adults invited to the party and so on.

The development of fantasy in play from fragments to sequences, from isolated imitations to connected narrative, should have taken place by the age of five, though it will certainly not stop at the age of five—if, in fact, it ever stops.

Some of these sequences or narratives will last a whole morning or even for several mornings, the play being carried over from one day to the next quite deliberately and this illustrates an important step forward in a child's intellectual development.

One morning, two four-year-olds decided that a nylon net shopping bag was a fishing net and that they would go fishing with it. The following day, they saw the shopping bag again and were immediately reminded of the 'fishing net' incident. 'Let's go fishing again!' they said, and used some chairs to make an imaginary boat. The 'boat' was an extension of the play sequence of the previous day, and it seems likely that, by using the ideas, the 'concepts' mastered earlier, children can reach out further into new experiences. By repeating and extending the uses of playthings, we eventually establish a means of re-creating these things and events in our minds without those things being actually there. We are beginning to 'conceptualise', or to 'think in pictures' and to associate these pictures, firstly as they were originally used, and secondly, in entirely new ways. Thus, the children remembered they had used the nylon shopping bag as a 'fishing net' and then extended the idea of using it on a 'boat'. This is the true use of a fantasy in play and without it we could not begin to think at all and we should certainly never learn to read.

Facets of fantasy

So, at around five years, children are making ships from chairs and boxes, and sailing to imaginary islands with real or concocted names. They will play at visits to hospitals, life in the home, build bridges with pieces of wood, bath the 'baby', search for monsters. In fact, any item of information which they are trying to assimilate and digest will be food for fantasy in play. In all these activities, they are exploring and discovering not only how the world works, but how they 'tick' as individuals, learning their limits and their capabilities. Obviously, it helps if they have a brother or sister or a friend to play with. Adults, though they may be ever so willing, are not always accepted as playmates by children. And lack of a playmate leads to a very common feature of the under-five's play activity which frequently causes parents some anxiety. This feature is the creation of the imaginary 'playmate'.

I remember being asked by one worried father about this, because he thought his four-year-old daughter was, as he put it, 'going barmy!' She was living in a fantasy world most of the time, and since he failed to appreciate the necessity for this type of play, he felt that the child was living out a whole mass of lies. He admitted quite openly that he just did not understand it.

There was another case of a small boy, whom I knew well, who lived most of his days with a character called 'Kingwee', a name which he had vaguely heard his mother use when going to a supermarket. 'Kingwee' was the nearest he could get to the actual name. On one occasion I tried to enter his world of 'Kingwee' and said that I could see this imaginary friend in a flower.

'You can't see him!' he said indignantly, and no amount of pressing would make him let me into his private world of fantasy and share it with me.

I think this latter example shows how much an under-five needs another child as a sounding board for his 'personal fantasy play' in which he is completely involving his voice, body, mind and feelings, in fact, his total personality. In 'projected play', on the other hand, he can use toys to talk to and handle, but in 'personal play' he is so *personally* involved that if there is no other child to be involved with him, he will probably create one.

It is, perhaps, worth pointing out here that, in this sense of inventing people, novelists and playwrights are creating 'playmates' and we call these writers 'creative'. It could be, then, that parents who are worried about their child's imaginary playmates might consider him 'creative' rather than 'barmy'.

Nevertheless, the imaginary playmate should fade out when a child reaches the age of seven and over because, by this time, he is able to distinguish between fantasy and reality. In fact, he will want to know about *real* things, *real* people and *real* events. Sometimes, however, particularly in the case of the lonely and only child, the phenomenon of invented playmates will continue for a while and then parents should try to make provisions and opportunies for their child to play with other *real* children, as they ought to do at every stage in their child's life. And in providing these opportunites, when parents find it impossible to do so themselves, the playgroup or nursery school can play a decisive part in developing a child's personality and ability to cope with life.

Fantasy play, or fantasy in play, serves to develop the emotions and the intellect in fairly specific ways, whereas physical development is apparent in every activity, as for example, when a child uses mainly his hands in 'projected play' or his whole body in 'personal play'.

There are two very practical and fundamental points to be made about parents' and teachers' attitudes towards fantasy in play.

Adult attitudes towards fantasy

Firstly, we must remember that play is totally absorbing and involves the child completely. Because of this, we should try to 'ease' a child out of the world of play he has created and in which he is temporarily living. By 'easing' I mean that we should try to enter this world and, if the child will let us, bring him back with us. On one occasion I had been working with some children who were all playing at being cats. I wanted the playing to come to an end and I asked the children to sit on their chairs. One little girl either refused or failed to hear or just had no wish to sit down. I tried going into her fantasy world myself, and said: 'Come on, pussy, sit down please!' And with a little 'miaow' she did.

Children, like animals, react violently to sudden, jerky movements or noise and they need time for their play to run down and fade away. Hurried movements by adults in order to get toys cleared away can cause great mental as well as physical disturbance in the form of tantrums and outbursts of temper. Young children need time to stop what they are doing, especially if they are completely involved in a piece of fantasy play. It is very difficult to stop running in your tracks: it is just as difficult to stop 'fantasising' at the snap of your fingers. So, although it may mean having more patience than you thought possible, do give children time to let their play come to an end. In the long run, it will help everyone to keep their tempers.

Secondly, when older children start to ask whether a piece of fantasy is actually true, that is to say, when they are beginning to be objective about their play and the distinction between fantasy and reality is clear-cut, we have to give some answer.

I think the answer lies in what I have already hinted at, namely, in art. So if a child wants to know whether a dragon really exists, the answer is that he does in the story, very much as he might do in a play in the theatre. I call this process of explanation 'de-fantasising'. The method usually works and answers some awkward questions, like 'Is it real?' or 'Is it true?' We do not want to destroy the magic too soon in life, and, in any case, we can all accept the truth of something 'in the book' or 'on the stage', even if we know what we read or see is not real.

Curiously enough, whereas a child of three may not be able to separate play from life, by the age of seven or eight, there is usually little doubt in the child's mind as to what is 'real' and what is 'pretend', unless, of course, fantasy in play has been denied or ridiculed by parents either deliberately or unconsciously. In this case, though not inevitably so, we could have a potential problem on our hands in terms of personality or slow learning.

Clearly, then, fantasy in play is a very necessary ingredient in the first five years of a child's life—and very possibly beyond. Parents and teachers, in their respective ways, need to provide a secure environment in which children can have the chance to develop the fantasy of 'disjointed bits of pretence' into the 'consistent sequences of make-believe'. This must be done at the child's pace, in his own time not ours, and we should never attempt to push children too hard, particularly on the intellectual level. For without fantasy in play, a child could be permanently deprived of one facet of life's experience. In the world of fantasy, of trial and error, it is symbolic thought, conceptualising or 'thinking in pictures' which is a prerequisite for the development of speech and eventually of reading. In the next chapter, we shall look at what I call language play.

4   Language play

Helping a child to develop his spoken language is one of the most important things any parent or teacher can do. In the home, however, since mother usually spends far more time than father with her pre-school child, she is likely to be more responsible for this process than he is. Naturally, this does not mean that she has to accept all the responsibility for her child's learning to speak. Every conversation a child has with adults, whether inside or outside the home, will affect his speech in some way, just as the children he plays with will also affect the development of his speech patterns or style. And style, which is concerned with vocabulary, grammar and accent, is something we all acquire even though we are not aware of it. Anyone's speech is bound to be influenced by the speech style of people in a particular geographical area and of those with specific social backgrounds.

Gradually, a child discovers that in his society he needs to accept some of the speech patterns of the people he meets and to reject others. And though it is a somewhat delicate issue in these democratic days, it is nevertheless true that the acceptance or rejection of certain aspects of these patterns or styles will be controlled to a great extent by the child's social environment, which in the first and formative years will be principally shaped by his own family.

One of the questions we shall have to look at is the kind of spoken language we think a child should use, and whether we ought to encourage any special form of speaking, or merely allow a child to pick up speech styles as he goes along without interference from us. There are many parents who take this latter course and do nothing about helping children's speech mainly because they feel it quite unnecessary to do so. In any case, they might say, 'Is there a right and wrong way to speak?'

Inevitably this raises the thorny question as to what 'correct' spoken English sounds like. We all have our own ideas about it, depending to some extent on the part of the country we come from. Nobody quite knows the answer to the question of 'correctness', even if there is such a thing, but there is no doubt that the language of a child's family group will influence the vocabulary, grammar and pronunciation of his own speech.

In practice, a child usually manages to compromise between his inventive use of language and the conventions of speech in his society. In fact, all children have at least three speaking styles: one for the home, one for school, and one for the playground. And part of the whole process of growing up and being educated is learning how and when to use a style of speech which is appropriate to a particular social situation.

There is no need to stress how vital speech is to any human being. A child who lacks fluency or who has little or no speech is unable to express his emotional and physical needs in words, and this can be very frustrating both for the child and for the parents. Because he can not draw attention to himself or make himself understood in any other ways, he may resort to crying or kicking up a tantrum. Uncontrolled screaming or stamping on the floor, which appear like outbursts of senseless aggression, quite often disappear when a child can tell us what he wants or what is worrying him. Screams and tantrums are usually distress signals that something is wrong, but they seldom indicate exactly what it is, whether it concerns cutting a tooth, a pain in the tummy or being left alone for a while. Yet as soon as a child has learned elementary speech, he can tell us about his particular problem more precisely, and he has no need to make a noisy and irritating fuss.

Moreover, without adequate speech, a child cannot test the

meaning of new words against the ideas he has already formed and which very possibly do not coincide with the meaning we give to them as adults. As Jean Piaget points out, this testing of new words is vital in forming new ideas or concepts, especially about life and living. These are particularly difficult notions for a child and do not always have the same meaning for an under-five as they do for adults. We shall be coming back to this question of life and living in a later chapter.

Though the development of speech is so important, it can never be forced. Speech has to grow naturally and like any living thing—and speech is certainly very much 'alive'—it needs certain conditions if it is to grow into maturity. Though parents can provide most of these conditions, they sometimes fail to do so, mainly because they do not know what these conditions are and how necessary they are for language development.

Two of the most important of these conditions are, firstly, conversation, and secondly, providing situations which stimulate conversation. Quite simply, we need to talk to children about

Talking to children about anything and everything is important.

anything and everything, and in this chapter, we shall be discussing the importance of spoken language to a young child and suggesting ways of encouraging its development. Before doing this, however, we must try to get rid of a few misconceptions about speech and the part it plays in pre-reading activities for under-fives.

Parents often believe that the quicker their children learn to speak, the sooner they learn to read; and reading, as I pointed out earlier, is held up as a yardstick by which parents' rather than children's prestige is measured. Indeed, some parents attach a great deal of prestige to their four-year-old who can read and write his own name before going to full-time school, and his ability to do this gives a sense of one-up-manship over the parent whose five-year-old is unable to distinguish a single letter.

Perhaps this sounds cynical, but it is unfortunately true. So it is worth trying to lay an old ghost about teaching under-fives to read. We would never ask a four-year-old to walk 16 kilometres. And if we are wise, we shall not subject children to emotional experiences, such as they might see on TV programmes, for which they are not emotionally ready. So we should not try to make a child read when he is intellectually unready.

The concept of 'reading readiness' relates to the time when a child, often quite suddenly, begins to read. Learning to read is rather like learning to ride a bicycle. One moment you fall off and the next you have mastered the trick of balancing without realising it. The age of 'reading readiness' varies from child to child, though we seldom find an under-five ready for reading, despite what parents may claim. Admittedly, *some* children who are rising five will be ready for reading and may even be able to do so, but in general, it is *spoken* not *written* language which the pre-school child needs. And I would suggest that reading schemes designed for two-year-olds should be avoided. One of these curious schemes appeared some years ago and received a great deal of publicity. Its major fault was that it did not take into account the difference between a child's repeating a word and understanding it. For example, the scheme required mother to hold up a card in front of her labelled 'Daddy'. If her child did associate the apparent meaning with the word, a very odd confusion could result. For under-fives, then, parents and teachers should concentrate on developing fluent speech and confidence in conversation.

Speech as play

Acquiring speech is really a facet of play, and in the previous chapters I have briefly mentioned how children play with sounds and words, first by imitating what they hear and then shuffling and sorting them out into patterns until they can eventually put words together into sentences. I believe this whole process is a form of play and if we do not see it in this way, we shall probably expect too much of children in their mastery of language. Or, more likely, we shall be misled into believing that children actually understand what they are saying. In the early stages of language play, saying words will be purely imitation. Only gradually does the meaning associated with the words being said become apparent. Even then, we shall sometimes find children using words in their own private way. Just as a child will tell us that a picture he has painted is of a sick teddy, though it may be quite unrecognisable to an adult, so he may repeat a word in all kinds of contexts, merely because he likes the sound of it. Understanding the meaning of a word as well as being able to pronounce it takes time, and it seems that the ability to say words develops quicker than the intellectual ability to comprehend them.

Obviously, lack of speech is a serious handicap to children, especially in their social contacts and their need to communicate with the world around them. Communication obviously takes place in conversation, and this leads us to look more closely at the first of the conditions I suggested as necessary for the development of speech.

The value of conversation in developing speech

There is no substitute for conversation if we want to help children to gain fluency in speech. In conversation we shall be introducing new words, some of which a child will understand, and some of which he will not, but there is no need to keep to very simple words. Children can manage quite difficult words and we should never underrate their intelligence. BBC television's *Magic Roundabout*, referred to earlier, is an excellent example of the way to treat conversation with under-fives. Eric Thompson's dialogue recognises the intelligence of young children, that they can pronounce and sometimes understand quite difficult words like 'mollusc' and so on. In conversation, never laugh at a child because he uses a funny word or is unable to pronounce a word properly. Always accept seriously what they say and talk to them as naturally as you would talk to your own friends.

In the conversation we have with children we are not only introducing new words but also establishing sentence patterns like the simple question, answer and statement types. And this involves a great deal more than merely being able to speak a few sentences. For spoken language is not the only way we can communicate with people.

Visual signals like waving a hand, winking an eye, smiling, putting out one's tongue and so on are all signals which we learn to interpret and respond to in the appropriate way. In fact, each of these special signals belongs to a definite situation. We might smile brightly at the bank manager or the man who reads the gas meter, but unless we know them both very well, we are hardly likely to wink at them!

Speech tones

Similarly in speaking, we have to learn how to respond to particular speech patterns or styles according to the situation in which something is said and the tone of voice used in saying it. For example, we need to know when to say 'Hello!' and when to say in an American style 'Hi!', or when to be more formal with a complete stranger, Hence we should not only be concerned with words and sentences, but also with helping children to experience, interpret and respond to what the language experts call 'linguistic overtones'—and there are a great many of them.

For instance, a simple statement like 'This is a beautiful book' can be turned into a question merely by raising the voice at the end of the sentence. As adults we are continually using this trick in our conversations, but young children will not hear this at first. Incidentally, I have found this particular conversational trick one that causes immigrant children special difficulty. And from my own experience of teaching in various tropical areas, I know that people for whom English is a second language do not find it at all easy to distinguish between a statement and a question, if the question is indicated only by a change in intonation. 'Do you like this book?' prompts an answer 'Yes' or 'No'. But the question put like this: 'You do like this book?', which can be shown in print by the question mark and in speech by a rising tone of voice at the end of the sentence, has to be heard and learnt by experience.

Apart from these examples of learning sentence patterns and sentence tones, the actual sound of the voice when we speak to children is extremely important. When mother says 'No!' in an unconvincing way, her child may think she means the opposite, because she often says 'No' and then gives in. The temper tantrum in a shop, when mother has refused to buy an iced lolly for her child, could be due to all those times in the past when 'No' has only been a lead up to 'Yes'. The child has learnt this whether we like it or not, so 'No' must really mean 'No' and it must be said with a decisive tone of voice. Moreover, 'No' must be backed up by a definite refusal to give in. Any parent or teacher who says 'No' in an unconvincing way and then allows a child to do or get what he wants is storing up trouble. Always try to mean exactly what you say.

Speech and society

There are other aspects of children's conversation which can be embarrassing to the parent or any adult who does not appreciate the stages in a child's social development. For example, never be upset by the directness and honesty of children's speech. It takes time for a child to know when he can say, 'I don't like Mrs. Smith' and when he should not. 'Language manners', as I like to call them, help us to live in comparative peace with each other, and I shall be discussing this question of manners and social conventions in a later chapter.

But we can make sure that children follow the simple patterns of speech conventions like 'hello', 'good-bye', 'please' and 'thank you'. Parents and teachers should realise that children need to learn what these conventions are. They should also realise that what might seem a deliberate insult is only natural curiosity on the part of the child. It is little use telling him he is being rude if he asks why Mrs. Smith wears funny hats or has big feet. He is not being rude, but merely curious. Under-fives are seldom, if ever, deliberately insulting.

Nevertheless, children can be embarrassing when they ask certain questions. Yet their continual 'Whys?' are a source of conversation. Naturally, their questions can be trying as well as embarrassing, because they cannot always cope with the answers, but to destroy a child's curiosity through impatience with his questions might destroy some of his ability to learn.

So in order to cope with the embarrassment of the questions a child asks or the comments he makes, parents need to cultivate a 'dead-pan' reaction, one which is not visibly shocked. By twisting one's own answers around, it is possible to steer a child into accepting some of the social conventions we have been mentioning. Perhaps I can illustrate this problem of 'social speech' with an example which actually happened to me. The example could be repeated many times in slightly different words.

I arrived in a playgroup and was greeted by a 'rising five'. The dialogue went something like this:

Child : What you come for? (No use saying 'what a rude boy!')

I : To see you. (This always seems to work and it is at least partly true.)

Child : What for? (Again, no point in saying the child is rude to ask.)

I : Well, I thought it would be nice to see you again. (Pause)

Child : What's your name? (Many parents and some teachers are embarrassed by this directness.)

I : Mr. Baker. What's yours? (This is fair; he has asked me, so I can ask him.)

Child : Robin.

I : Hello, Robin.

Child : Hello. (There is often another pause here, while the child weighs up the situation and decides, like adults making a new acquaintance, whether to develop the meeting or not. Usually, a tiny hand takes mine or tugs my coat.)

Child : Come and see my pictures. (And I am led away.)

Now the directness of the child's questions in this piece of true conversation could cause offence to anyone who is not aware of what a child is trying to do, or that he has yet to learn an appropriate style of address. Using a dead-pan response, we must try to answer as courteously as possible and hope that mutual respect will grow.

What we cannot do is tell a child he is rude for asking questions, especially about why a visitor has come to the house or the class-room. After all, the child is only expressing genuine curiosity. Eventually, and only very slowly over the years, we can hope to show children, by our own courtesy in dealing with them and by listening to them without interrupting their conversation, how to appreciate the social situation they are in and the style of language, its conventions and so forth, to use in it.

So we should always accept children's chatter and treat it seriously. Give them time to express themselves and never interrupt them. We have no reason to condemn children for interrupting adults' conversations if we do it to them.

Helping children to develop speech

The first condition, then, for helping children to develop their speech is to enter into conversation with them as much as possible. In this conversation, we must give positive meanings to words and distinct patterns to sentences, so that children will be gradually learning not only the vocabulary and grammar by listening and repeating, but also the conventions of speech and the overtones which are as much a part of spoken language as words and sentences.

The second condition concerns ways of stimulating conversa-tion and I have already hinted at some of these in talking about conversation in general. But there are several things we can do to help. It used to be said that the newspaper prevented conversa-tion; now television is the scapegoat, but whatever reasons we give for lack of conversation, if we really want children to talk freely and express themselves clearly, stimulating situations must be provided.

Talk, talk, talk, is the key to speech development. I remember one case of a three-year-old, whose only means of drawing attention to himself were to tap on a grown-up's leg or just grunt! His speech was almost non-existent and he was recommended to a playgroup, mainly because he was suffering from under-stimulation in the home. He needed people to listen to and to talk to. After a few months, speech began to develop, because the other children did not respond to taps and grunts. He had to speak to make himself understood.

A similar curious situation is often seen in a family where the youngest child relies on the older children to mediate between his own needs and his parents' responses. The children know what he wants and the parents accept this situation, not realising that they are preventing the youngest child from learning to speak.

So do talk to your child about anything and everything. There are stimulating situations in everyday events in the home. Such matters as the postman being late. Has he brought us any letters? Look out of the window and see if you can see the milkman in the street. Maybe you will be in the kitchen, so tell your under-five why you are adding water to the pastry, and what happens if you don't.

Pretend you need to know the time. Ask him to look at the clock and show you with his fingers where the hands of the clock are pointing. Then say: 'That means half-past eleven'. Soon, he will be telling you without using his fingers. And, incidentally, this is an example of the sensori-motor learning process in which movement reinforces the formation of concepts.

Books, of course, are great stimulators. Try to spend a short time each day looking at a book together. Bedtime is an obvious moment for this to happen. Talk about some of the things in the book. What are the people wearing? What colour is the lady's coat? Is it the same as mine? Pictures, too, can help to stimulate conversation in the same way. And, whenever possible, any kind of outing is most valuable, because there will be so many new things to talk about, whether it is the flowers in the lane or the brightly-coloured cans of food in the supermarket. In fact, in the latter case, you can talk about what you need to buy or what you will cook for lunch, or tea or supper. Admittedly, some of the conversations will go over his head, but this does not matter in the least, because the sentence patterns will be forming in his head and the new words will be making some sort of impact on him.

The two main conditions for encouraging children's speech are conversation and stimulation. And if there is nothing much to talk about then conversation can not take place effectively, which leads us into saying something about the controversial issue of speech styles associated with particular social groups.

To speak of class differences in these days is bound to raise many objections. No doubt most people believe that a classless society would be an ideal world to live in. But however much we may regret it, class distinctions exist, though not in the traditional terms of upper, middle and working. Sometimes a person's class is now defined according to the manual or mental work done by himself or his parents, the neighbourhood where he lives, education and so on, and any or all of these factors add up to what some people now call life-styles.

Language and life-style

Each of us has a life-style, though we may not be aware of it, and this life-style, unless we deliberately reject it for some reason, will be reflected in the life-style of our children. And this is where the question of language, both written and spoken, comes in, since home environment is bound to affect children's speech in terms of vocabulary and fluency. In homes where children are not surrounded by stimulating experiences and hence where there is little to talk about, conversation between parents and between parents and children is frequently almost non-existent. Family speech in these homes is usually concerned with the essentials of day-to-day living. There is, therefore, little opportunity for language play, exploring new words, new ideas, new ways of saying things, so speech development is seriously restricted.

A great deal of work has been done on the relationship between language and social class. Perhaps the best known name in this field is that of Basil Bernstein, who distinguishes two speech styles, one associated with the middle class and the other with the working class.

In the working class, Bernstein claims, conversation in the home tends to be in short sentences with commands accompanied by gestures and facial expressions. The visual signals are as significant as the words themselves. Little reasoning power is required at an intellectual level, conversation being based more on emotional responses. In making these points, I must stress that there is no suggestion of a lower intelligence in this group, but because the stimulating experiences are fewer, there is no necessity for new words and new means of expressing any new ideas.

The middle class, on the other hand, depends much more on logical connections between statements, and the visual signals in facial or hand gestures are not so important.

There is general agreement that Bernstein over-simplifies the issue, but it does seem true that one class can be distinguished from another, and that a child from one social class with its particular characteristics of language might find it difficult to adjust to the language style of another. So a child who comes from a home where there are few experiences to talk about, and homes like this are by no means associated only with the lower income groups, is clearly at a disadvantage.

As a result of research into language and social class, Denis and Judy Gahagan have produced a language enrichment scheme entitled *Telltales* which could certainly be used with under-fives, either in groups or with individuals. The series consists of four sets of picture story cards and children build up the sequence of events in the stories told by the pictures. *Telltales*, therefore, generates conversation and encourages logical thought.

To illustrate the difficulty of adjustment between the language of home and that of school or playgroup I can describe something which actually happened. Leila Berg's *Nipper* books are intended to appeal to those children whose speech style is that of the lower income groups—the 'working class'. But a problem can arise when these stories are used with children from other social groups.

One story, entitled *Well I never*, opens with these sentences: ' "He pinched my bike." "No, I never." "Yes, you did." ' When this story was told to a group of mainly middle class playgroup children, one commented: 'We don't say "pinched". We say stole.' And I suppose he did, but whether he would say it in every situation or not is another matter.

We shall be discussing the language of stories in the next chapter, but it seems to me that we have to decide how appropriate the language used in a particular story is by taking into account the various social backgrounds of the children and we also have to understand our purpose in telling a story with a distinctive speech style. The BBC *Jackanory* series uses story-tellers with different regional accents in order to overcome any special emphasis on what used to be called 'BBC English', which had a strong 'southern' flavour in it.

Two points follow from all this. Firstly, we should be aware of the style of speech, including its accent, regional or otherwise, which we are using and which our children are also likely to use. And secondly, and this is perhaps more relevant to teachers and playgroup workers, we should not deny children the experience of exploring speech styles other than their own.

It does help, of course, if each identifiable group is brought into contact with others and some schools and playgroups will draw on a fairly wide range of social groups.

But whether in playgroup or the home, contact between these groups can be made by letting children explore their different speech styles. There are two main ways of doing this: firstly, and more informally, by just letting children listen and talk to other children; and secondly, by letting them listen to storytellers with regional accents on radio and television, or by reading stories about different social groups to them. To a child who makes a comment like 'We don't say that' we can only say that some people do.

Finally, to return to those two conditions I suggested were necessary for the development of children's speech, namely, conversation and stimulation. Cultural deprivation, as the sociologists call it, is not confined to any one income group. It means failure to surround children with experiences which can provide talking points. If parents talk only about the absolute essentials of everyday life, their children will never develop the fluency and flexibility of speech necessary for learning to read and write and above all to communicate in rational language rather than aggressive and violent gestures.

5 Story play

People have told stories to each other ever since speech began. And then, after alphabets were invented and it became possible to write a language, many legends and folk tales were written down—not that an alphabet is essential to recording a story. The famous cave paintings in France and Spain, for example, relate a narrative that is thought to be about war and the way the tribe found its food. And, of course, the picture comics, in which minimal reading, if any, is required, show that this form of story-telling is far from dead.

Indeed, because it still is very much alive, it forms one of the most important ways in which a non-reading under-five can learn to follow a story or gain pieces of information. By interpreting the signs and symbols of the picture language, he may be discovering certain facts about life, but he is also being prepared for the technique of reading a printed page.

Printed story books for children can be placed in two major categories. Firstly, there are those that children can read for themselves, and, secondly, there are those designed to be told or read *to* children. For the very young child, the latter are obviously the most relevant, though to the non-reading under-five, books with clear, simple pictures in strong colours are a very useful means of introducing him to the value of books and to the technique of recognising shapes and patterns, a technique that has to be mastered before learning to read.

But for older children who can read there is a time and place for their being read to as well as for reading by themselves. In a later chapter, we shall be looking at some examples of various types of children's books in order to see what themes are likely to appeal to children and how best they are presented in story books and information books. In this chapter, we shall concentrate on the functions of stories and the need every society in the world has for myth, parable and legend.

The functions of stories

None of us ever really grows out of either reading or listening to stories. The serialised novels or the 'morning story' on the radio witness to the perennial fascination of the storyteller's craft.

In fact, the story world is essentially a world that lies parallel to our own, a world where everything is in order, and we can compensate for the things we have lost in real life. Stories assure us that all is temporarily well with the world of reality, and that, despite what can happen to us later, at least for the moment our peace of mind is secured by the sure knowledge that the story-teller will create some sort of order out of the chaos that sometimes seems to surround us.

Discussing the particular functions of fairy tales, J. R. R. Tolkien, who was mentioned earlier in connection with fantasy play, suggests that fairy tales serve three main purposes: they offer us 'Recovery, Escape and Consolation'.

'Recovery (which includes return and renewal of health) is a re-gaining of a clear view.' It is like seeing things anew with their original wonder and freshness, so that the world itself with its trees and flowers, its clouds and sun, its wind and rain, its animals, insects, birds and people come truly alive for us once again.

'Escape', Tolkien continues, 'is as a rule very practical, and may even be heroic.' It is not deserting the world, as some critics might think, but an escape from prison, the confinement imposed upon us by the chaos of the actual world. Even more profound is Tolkien's suggestion that human beings need to make contact with their beginnings, with their lost innocence, with a time when there was real contact with the world of living things, its birds and animals, trees and plants. Not for nothing have some experts on mythology pointed out that the story of 'Paradise Lost' is common to many peoples throughout the world. And how many stories begin: 'Once upon a time there was a beautiful garden and then . . .' And so we tend to escape into the story-teller's world where animals and children talk to each other, where we recover something of our lost sense of wonder and in doing so restore our emotional balance.

And so, finally, we find consolation in the joy of the happy ending. '. . . this joy is not essentially "escapist" nor "fugitive". In its fairy-tale "other world" setting, it is a sudden and mira-culous grace never to be counted on to recur; it denies universal final defeat giving a fleeting glimpse of Joy, Joy beyond the walls of the world . . .'

But even if there is no 'happy ever after' ending the story-teller's kingdom remains one in which we do not have to live ourselves and we know that, despite its tragedies and upheavals, the whole pattern of the narrative is safe in the writer's hands. And, in some curious way, the story can become a parable of human existence, with the writer a symbol of divine providence.

There are, of course, especially in these rational and scientific days, many people who criticise the 'escapism' and fantasy of folk and fairy tale in particular and the mythical or legendary story in general, because, they claim, it prevents children from facing up to the real problems of life. But as T. S. Eliot once remarked, 'Human kind cannot bear very much reality', and with this remark and with Tolkien's belief in the need for recovery, escape and consolation most psychologists and sociologists would agree, for the story, by assuring us that all is temporarily well, is in effect a form of fantasy play. Here it is worth quoting the sociologist Peter Berger, who sees any story told by a mother to comfort her child as a facet of play. 'Joyful play', writes Berger, appears to suspend or bracket the reality of our "Living towards death" . . . It is this curious quality, which belongs to all joyful play, that explains the liberation and peace such play provides.

54

In early childhood, of course, the suspension is unconscious, since there is as yet no consciousness of death. In later life play brings about a beatific reiteration of childhood. When adults play with genuine joy, they momentarily retain the deathlessness of childhood.'

Now these are high claims for the function of play in general, but I hope it became clear in previous chapters that play is as natural as sleep and as necessary as dreams. This is especially true for under-fives who are coping with an enormous amount of information flooding into them from the world outside. In order to cope with the often confusing, frequently conflicting information they are continually receiving about the world, these children need a fantasy world into which they can escape for recovery and consolation. And I believe that, although we are all in need of fantasy from the youngest to the oldest, fantasy is particularly necessary and relevant to the very young child. And stories and storytelling are aspects of 'fantasy play'.

The world of play is, in effect, a 'dramatised' story, a parallel world, or an acted parable of life, where, because the children are in control of it themselves, everything is ordered exactly as they wish it to be. The story serves a similar purpose, though it is obviously less physically demanding than other forms of play. Moreover, the story is created by someone else, not the children themselves; it is, in fact, an imaginary world into which they are invited by the writer or storyteller.

The ability to imagine or fantasise is uniquely human and without it we might even lose our humanity; for human beings can create fantasy worlds of potentialities and possibilities, and, thus, as a specific form of play, the story assumes considerable importance in terms of its power to humanise as well as its appeal as straightforward entertainment. This particular purpose of the story is what Tolkien meant by 'Recovery, Escape and Consolation', because it is by the telling of myths, legends and parables, that we are led into a world where, despite the anguish of living (not by any means confined to adult life, for children experience many terrors and many anxieties) everything is presented as if it were in order. The actual world may then begin to make sense, because our sense of emotional balance has been restored by our entering storyland and identifying ourselves with those who meet and deal effectively with anxiety, fear and guilt.

Categories of stories according to their functions

This leads us to look more closely at the specific functions of stories, which, as I see them, have three main objects. The first function is 'mythological' and tries to relate us to existence itself; the second is really parabolic and deals with the more personal and particular problems of life, whilst the third gives children the opportunity of hearing about typical experiences in the daily life of any child. The delight and satisfaction produced by the last kind of story seems to derive from children's recognition of events and people like themselves. Apart from the specific functions of stories, there is, of course, the sheer pleasure of the narrative itself and we should never underestimate the importance of the pleasure and joy which both storyteller and listener share.

Mythological folk and fairy tales

In mythological stories, then, we are coming to terms with the meaning of existence. For children, these stories will often be the 'Where did I/it come from?' type. For example, a fundamental puzzle facing every race and tribe in the world is that of creation, and the question 'How did it all begin?'. The storyteller tries to answer the question long before the scientist offers an explanation. A Chinese narrator might say: 'Well, once upon a time chaos was like a hen's egg and it broke open. The heavy parts became the earth and the light parts made the sky.' Curiously enough, the myth of the primeval world egg is common to various eastern mythologies and certainly not confined to China.

Or someone asks: 'Where did our people come from?' And a Japanese storyteller relates how once upon a time a great carp lay asleep under the sea. When he awoke, he thrashed about wildly and caused huge tidal waves which washed up the islands of Japan. Obviously, these are not scientific explanations, but attempts to absorb the inexplicable into patterns of human thought. In the fantasy land of story play, anything can happen because the rules are laid down by the storyteller and are accepted by the listeners or readers. And, incidentally, the same things happen in more active play where children make up their own temporary rules which they keep as long as they want their world of play to continue. The ending of all forms of active fantasy play corresponds to the shutting of the book or the end of the storyteller's tale.

Perhaps because of our technologically dominated way of life, we have lost those mythological ways of thinking. According to the psychologist, Carl Jung, this failure to manipulate symbols in fantasy and dream, whether in active or story play, has led to a loss of the ability to create and organise symbols which satisfy the deep longings within all of us for order and meaning in life. It is in stories that the imaginative, creative urge in human life has free play and events that might have actually happened are manipulated by the storyteller into a pattern that has meaning and satisfaction for him. But the significance and meaning which the creator of the story has discovered are also communicated in the telling of it to others. In story play, we are given the possibility of coming to terms with reality, with the hopes and fears, the joys and sorrows of actual life. A story opens up an imaginative world where order prevails despite the many puzzling and frightening events it frequently portrays. And stories do so by presenting us with fictional, legendary and mythical characters with whom we can identify and in whose struggles and tasks we share. By such means, then, we are able to work out, or rather to 'play out' the real-life problems we have to face and solve.

To illustrate the ways in which a story can help children cope with their terrors and their guilt by using an imaginary scapegoat let us look at Maurice Sendak's *Where the Wild Things Are*.

The story begins: 'The night Max wore his wolf suit and made mischief of one kind and another his mother called him "WILD THING!" and Max said "I'LL EAT YOU UP!" so he was sent to bed without eating anything.' Plainly, this is based on the common behaviour of young children who 'make mischief' and then receive some form of punishment for it. Hence they feel guilty because they have apparently lost the love of a parent. Somehow, that love has to be restored, but none of us likes to admit guilt. We all try to shift the blame on to someone else, so Max wears his wolf suit, as a kind of personal disguise. In effect, everything that happens is happening not to Max, but to the boy pretending to be a wolf!

Maurice Sendak cleverly uses a child's ability to slip easily from fantasy to reality by describing how Max's room grows into a forest and then into an ocean on which he sails 'in and out of weeks and almost over a year to where the wild things are'.

At first, all Max's terrors of monsters and 'things that go bump in the night' are shown in the terrible roars and terrible teeth and terrible eyes and terrible claws of the strange creatures of fantasy. Then Max says: 'BE STILL!' and tames them with a magic trick of staring into all their yellow eyes without blinking once and 'they were frightened and called him the most wild thing of all and made him king of all wild things'.

So Max comes to terms with his fear and returns over the weeks and days of the ocean until he finds himself back in his own room 'where he found his supper waiting for him and it was still hot'. The implication of this last part of the story is that Max has been forgiven and has his food after all. Thus his terror (which might have made him naughty in the first place for all we know) his guilt and his anxiety have all been removed and his mother's love is restored. And incidentally, Max has also discovered what it is like to frighten as well as to be frightened.

A similar purpose, though in simpler terms, is served by one of the stories in the excellent collection called *Lucky Dip,* originally written by Ruth Ainsworth for the BBC's *Listen with Mother* programmes. Most of the stories concern a little boy, Charles, and one in particular deals with the guilt a child may feel at being cross and causing parental displeasure.

Charles is cross because the day is dull. He plays with monkey, one of his old, favourite toys and decides to go for a walk with him. During the walk, Charles tells monkey how cross he has been, and monkey agrees. Charles says he will never be cross again. Here, of course, we have the familiar technique of using a scapegoat as a kind of confessional. So a story can be a means of underlining anti-social behaviour and helping children to modify it. At the same time, by 'confessing' his bad temper to monkey, Charles—and perhaps any child who listens to the story —feels he is accepted by his mother once more.

Parabolic stories or fables with a moral

So far we have talked about the psychological functions of a story, some of which fringe on the religious. But young children can also derive considerable help in facing future events by meeting them first in stories. For example, a visit to hospital can be prepared for by telling children a story in which a child goes to the doctor. The effect of the story can be reinforced by playing out a future event of this kind with stethoscope and a simple doctor's kit in a form of drama or active play.

Preparation for the time when children leave home or play-group for school can also be made through stories. We should always remember that leaving the comparatively secure world of home or playgroup where mother is present or grown-ups are known can be, and frequently is, a very frightening experience for the five-year-old. If a story can be backed up with an actual visit to the school, so much the better.

I prefer to call stories of this type 'parabolic' or fables with a moral because they serve either as a preparation for possibly frightening situations or as a warning against potential dangers. Often these stories are concerned with animals, but clearly enough, the parallel is drawn between the fictitious animal world and human experience. An important effect of using animals as the basis of fables or parables is that the listener or reader is set at a greater imaginative distance from the events described than would be the case in a story only about humans. We know that these events could happen to us, but since they are happening to animals, we feel somewhat safer. Nevertheless, we still draw the intended moral conclusion. *Aesop's Fables* are, of course, the classic example of the parabolic type of story, but Dick Bruna's *Pussy Nell* or Helen Cresswell's *A House for Jones*, both of which will be discussed in a later chapter, serve a similar purpose. Before going any further, one point needs to be made about fables and parables.

Sometimes it may be helpful to use the name of an actual child as the name of the child mentioned in the story, so that he can identify with the character and share in the solution of his problems. At other times, we shall find a child not wishing to hear his own name mentioned in a story. In fact, he may become acutely embarrassed by it as one four-year-old, whose name was Patrick, became embarrassed when the story, *Patrick*, by Quentin Blake, was being read.

A possible reason for this embarrassment is that there is a curious reluctance on the part of all of us, but especially children, to give up our name. A name seems to be linked to our personality and, by broadcasting it, we subconsciously feel we are giving up something that is peculiarly ours. If a child is embarrassed and objects to his own name in a story, we should never laugh at him, but respect the objection and change the name. What we are doing is what Maurice Sendak makes Max do—put on a disguise!

Only in this case, it is the disguise of a name not a wolf suit.

Stories, then, because they relate to the world of play, serve the universal purpose of relating us to existence itself, and also to the more personal problems and particular fears of daily life. Broadly speaking, according to their content, stories can be either mythological and based on fantasy whose various functions, you may remember, included 'Escape, Consolation and Recovery'. Or they can be 'parabolic' dealing with more concrete problems and rooted in real-life situations. There is, however, a third type, which is neither 'fantastic' nor 'parabolic', but is concerned with ordinary life.

Stories of everyday life

In stories of this type no philosophical analogies are made and no moral conclusions are drawn. Their function is to reinforce the learning of certain facts about the child's world. Thus a child's experience of new information is given greater point and purpose as he listens to stories in which the events are similar to those he has already encountered.

The *Little Pete* stories by Leila Berg are excellent examples of the way to use typical real-life experiences in a story. They deal quite factually with such things as comparative sizes ('If a leaf goes into a matchbox, will a feather?') or with the difference between a boy and his shadow ('What happens when a road roller runs over a shadow?') or the textures of leaves as they can be felt in the prickles of holly compared with the softness of a feather. Obviously, some stories of the *Little Pete* type will need modification when being told to under-fives, but their general outline is perfectly suitable.

Very young children delight in hearing factual stories. They serve no obvious purpose and there are no ulterior motives in telling them except for enjoyment. But it may be that this enjoyment derives from the pleasure and satisfaction an under-five experiences when hearing about a child who lives very much as he does. Moreover, there is one point about stories in general and of this third type in particular which is worth making. It concerns the structure of the story or the way the narrative is put together.

The structure and language of stories

Structurally, depending on the method used to unfold the narrative, a story can reinforce the ultimate security offered by the play world. For example, children love the ritual of repetition, whether it is rhythmic stamping, spoon banging or repeating a word or sound. They especially love to hear the repetition of a word, phrase or incident in a story. Hearing a story exactly repeated seems to provide a sense of security in knowing what happens next. Young children do not need, as adults often do, the element of suspense in a story—rather the direct opposite. The effect of giving security by making what comes next predictable is preserved in many folk and fairy tales, where events or characters frequently appear in threes: for example the three bears, three billy goats, three tasks to perform and so on. It may be that the structure of repetition in 'three sizes' or 'three times' completes the triangle of the fundamental family relationships of father, mother and child. Whatever the explanation may be, children must have a story related in exactly the same way each time it is told. To disrupt the pattern is to destroy the security.

In terms of sentence structure, a story for a very young child should be absolutely simple without being patronising. The pattern of incident plus incident is ideal. The reason for this device is that it reflects the way young children tell their own tales, and perhaps this in turn reflects the way in which they put their own thoughts together. So they often say something like this: 'I got up *and* I had my breakfast *and* I went out *and* I played *and* I had my dinner *and* . . .' And so it goes on! A story that is based on this kind of structure with elements of repetition in the story itself will nearly always appeal to the under-fives.

Stories, then, are much more than 'entertainment', a means of passing time. They are absolutely necessary in helping us to meet and deal with life in all its puzzling and frightening aspects. To quote Harvey Cox: 'Fantasy is uniquely human. A hungry lion may dream about a zebra dinner but only man can mentally invent wholly new ways of living his life as an individual and as a species . . . fantasy is a form of play that extends the frontiers of the future'—and absorbs the experiences of the past, we might add, because children need to understand these experiences and to make them part of the fabric of their own lives.

Stories play a real part in this process, and although these may be high claims for fantasy in general and stories in particular, I firmly believe that stories have always had the functions we have been talking about. In the forms of myth, fairy tale and parable

I am sure they are essential to the sanity of the human race. So we should never forget the importance of what we are doing whenever we tell children a story, for in telling it we are not just entertaining children, but teaching them about life.

6 Role-play and dressing up

'Role-play' is a term sociologists have borrowed from the language of drama and which they now use to describe human behaviour in different situations. Like the word 'personality' which, as we shall see in a moment, is also derived from the language of the theatre, the term 'role-play' only goes to show how close all aspects of playing in life are to a play performed in a theatre. Peter Brook, the famous theatre director, points out this close relationship when he writes: 'It is not by chance that in many languages the word for a play and to play is the same'. Role-playing is really playing at life, and on the stage, of course, the actor has to learn to play many roles which he may never have experienced in his own life.

Dressing up is merely an aid to or reinforcement of the role we choose to play, whether on stage or in life. For example, whenever mother takes off her apron to serve coffee to visitors, she is changing her roles, from housewife to hostess, a slight but subtle difference! And most men put on different clothes for a night out. Usually we play the particular role that society expects of us in a given situation.

Many books on under-fives mention dressing up because it is

an essential facet of young children's play, whether at home, playgroup, nursery or first school. But few books deal with the underlying reasons why children delight in dressing up or with its value in the total learning process. So in this chapter, instead of listing practical hints on encouraging dressing-up play, we shall discuss some of these reasons. In fact, we shall see that role-play and dressing up are examples of what Peter Slade calls 'personal play' in which the whole person, that is the body, mind and emotions, is used.

Any form of play develops the personality of a child, and role-play and dressing up do so in a very special way. The word 'personality' comes from the Latin *persona*, a word used to describe the mask worn by Roman actors in the theatre. An actor could and often did wear many different masks in the course of a performance, and quick-change artists were just as popular then as they are now. Each time he changed his mask or *persona,* the actor changed his character or 'personality'. In this theatrical sense, a Roman actor could have as many 'personalities' as he had masks to wear. Similarly, our personality may not consist of one fixed set of characteristics, but a whole range of them. And it is part of the activity of play to try out these masks, *personae* or 'roles' and, like an actor using a mask to indicate the role he was playing on the Roman stage, we learn to shape our *persona* to the social situation we happen to be in at any given time.

In fact, we all play a different part in different situations and, like actors on the stage, we are continually adjusting our attitudes to them by creating roles to fit. Through language, which is one expression of our personality and is a means of communicating it to others, we have to discover how to make ourselves mesh with other people's personalities. By discovering what our range of *personae* really is and by accepting the disturbance of our personal patterns by other people's *personae* we are, in effect, learning how to live in society.

Of course, although we may possess this range of *personae,* there is something deep within us which seems to control and cause us to change masks, put on different faces in order to deal with various social situations. And this deep-seated control is what might be called our personality, which in its turn represents the sum total of all the faces or masks or roles we have learned to play.

It is precisely because there are such close associations between the concept of children's play and the theory and language of the theatre that I always try to avoid using a phrase like 'dramatic play' as if it were a distinct form of playing. I believe that *all* play is 'drama' or 'doing' to an under-five, and this is merely using the word 'drama' in its original sense. Hence, it seems unnecessary and confusing to describe, as many writers on the education of under-fives tend to do, some play as 'dramatic' and some as 'imaginative' and so on. Role-play is also drama and whether children use clothes or not to disguise themselves and represent other people or *personae*, dressing up is a reinforcement of their fantasy in which, as in all playing, they explore the various roles they observe in their ever-widening world.

To explain how role-playing works, we can take as an example the difference between our behaviour at home and at work, or in the case of children, how a child's behaviour and speech are seldom the same at home as they are at school. Eventually, we learn not only *how* to use these roles but also *when* to use them. Closely linked with role-playing is the use of language, which we discussed in an earlier chapter, and, as I pointed out then, it is vitally important for a child to experiment with speech patterns and to discover how to adapt his speech to different social conventions. The same thing is true of behaviour. We all have to learn certain conventions of behaviour, conventions that belong to our own society and culture and, at the same time, to respect the different social patterns and culture of other people. These matters are especially important for anyone who has to deal with mixed racial groups.

The value of role-playing

For children, the value of role-playing is obvious. Within the security of their play structures, either individually or in a group, they can explore roles which they have seen other people playing in real life. Some of these roles may be objectionable to us, and we may consequently describe a child's behaviour as anti-social, unkind, or even wicked. In these circumstances, a parent or teacher needs tolerance and understanding, for it is within these play sequences and in the disguise, *persona* or mask that children can experiment with and ultimately play out the evil or unpleasantness in their lives. With adults, the theatre, cinema or TV

Exploring domestic roles.

can often fulfil the same purpose, but, of course, such activities as group therapy and what is called 'psychodrama' do it more effectively, for the simple reason that the adult can actually play different roles and thus 'play out' just as a child plays out his fears and problems.

Naturally, all role-playing is not of this kind. Many roles are taken from home life, so that girls may play at being mother, who cooks, lays the table, prepares the meals, baths the baby and puts him to bed and so on. Boys will often play typically masculine roles like that of policeman, cowboy, soldier and, in these days. a spaceman. One or two curious and common features of the respective role-playing of boys and girls are worth noting.

Features of role-play

If you watch children playing, you will usually see that whereas girls play at being mothers for long spells, boys do not on the whole assume the father role nearly so frequently. The reason may be that young children spend far more time with their mother as a rule, and so are able to see and to imitate what she does. On the other hand, unless father works at or near home where children can watch and copy him, he is usually a person who goes out in the morning and comes home at night.

Another characteristic feature of role-playing in young children, which may result from the general social pattern of mother at home and father at work, is that boys frequently assume the role played by a girl in real life, but seldom, if ever, does a girl play a masculine role. Boys put on a girl's dress without any embarrassment. Whether psychiatrists would detect any sinister Freudian complex in this type of dressing-up play, I do not know. To me it seems much more likely that children are merely experimenting with roles they have observed, but have not yet clearly identified as those played by males and females in actual life. In fact, it may not be until around five or so that children begin to see the significance of physical differences between sexes. The possibility that father is made differently from mother, brother from sister begins to make its impact on the older under-fives and we occasionally see a girl's self-portrait equipped with a penis. Indeed, the experience of penis deprivation in a girl is quite common and should cause parents no alarm. It is the natural expression of curiosity about the body and parallels the dressing-up play in which sex roles are reversed.

The current trend towards the rejection of sex differentiation by means of clothing and length of hair is demanding an entirely different and frequently puzzled response from children in their learning about life. It may be that we have not sufficiently recognised the problems that changing social attitudes can cause them. One four-year-old boy, whose hair was shoulder-length, was poked in the stomach by a three-year-old girl who said 'You isn't a boy, you is a girl'. This sort of reaction results from the deep-seated, traditional attitudes towards differentiating the sexes by dress and appearance which many people have. On the whole, children prefer routine and stability in society. They like to know where they are regarding each other, or, putting the matter another way, they like to know 'who's who' and 'what's what'. Following a trend may be fashionable for adults who have already learned to distinguish their sex roles, but children can find it difficult and confusing. Playing out these roles can help children to form their own ideas about each other.

There is no reason why boys should not play at jobs traditionally done by girls. Boys can cook and sew, just as girls can do carpentry and mend cars. The main point to remember is that, having realised our possible role in life, we have then constructed the schemas mentioned in an earlier chapter, and against these schemas it is possible to explore further. Firstly, however, we all have to realise who we are. And for the under-five, this is, perhaps, the most important function of role-playing and dressing-up play.

Functions of dressing up

We can now go on to note some of the more specific purposes of dressing up in role-play. In the first place, it helps children to find an identity, a *persona* or personality which makes him or her a unique human being. Children construct this personality out of the various roles they play in early life. Eventually, then, the child has experienced a range of roles and from them has created his own persona which is not quite the same as anyone else's.

Secondly, dressing up often enables a shy, reserved child, especially if he is the only one in the family, to play more freely and easily with other children. As anyone who has ever worn a mask at a party or bonfire night will know, and as tribal witch doctors and fetish priests are well aware, we all tend to lose our inhibitions and become less self-conscious when wearing a mask, simply because our real identity is temporarily concealed. Similarly, a child becomes less inhibited and much more capable of communicating with others in co-operative play sequences if he wears some form of disguise.

Hats serve the same purpose as masks, and young children should have a few to experiment with, whilst a playgroup or nursery school should always have a large store of old hats. Some hats can be realistic replicas of the helmets and hats worn by firemen, policemen, soldiers, nurses and busmen. Mother's old hats are also useful. Though replicas serve their purpose, it is better still if mothers and fathers can pass on the real things when they no longer have any use for them. Real hats are better than plastic imitations, though, for obvious reasons, a real fireman's helmet would be a bit awkward to acquire and to wear!

Adults' hats may seem rather large for small children, but even

Dressing up as an aid to group play.

if the child is apparently unable to see from under a peaked cap, he is usually quite unconcerned himself. In fact, this is part of the wish for total disguise and also a variation of the familiar 'peek-a-boo' of play: 'If I can't see you, you can't see me!'

Sometimes children will play for a whole morning without taking a hat off. I have watched playgroup children, for example, put on a hat as soon as they arrive, then listen to stories, drink milk and engage in every possible activity from the beginning to the end of a session without taking their hats off. A hat, then, is the child's equivalent of a mask and there is a curious sense of being someone else, of unconsciously playing a role, when wearing it.

One very shy rising five about to go to first school was causing his mother great concern because of what she believed to be his excessive shyness. Very discreetly, I watched him one morning in his playgroup put on a policeman's helmet, and with two other boys, also wearing helmets, begin a play sequence that lasted throughout the playgroup session. Under the *persona* suggested by the helmet, he was a sergeant giving orders to his

Wearing cat suits and rabbit suits as disguises.

men. He worked out in discussion with his two companions the rules of the game and saw to it that they all kept them. He was, in effect, a different 'person', playing a role that he normally avoided.

The fact that he was wearing a policeman's helmet does not mean that he would eventually become a policeman. What it does mean is that by playing that particular role, he discovered his potential for co-operation and leadership. Indeed, he began to establish an identity of his own and this is one of the primary functions of play in general and of dressing-up play in particular. But first a child needs to explore a whole range of roles and then to incorporate various elements of each into his developing personality. Thus he takes a facet from this role and a facet from that as he gradually constructs his individual personality. We all go through this process as we explore many different roles and discover partly how they give us personal satisfaction and partly how they meet with the approval of the world at large. Sometimes, of course, the roles children choose to play meet with parental disapproval. This can cause a child to feel guilty for what he believes he has done to offend father or mother and to become anxious over what he may think is the loss of his parents' interest. This leads us to consider a third purpose in dressing-up play.

When wearing a hat or dress or complete cowboy outfit, catsuit or something similar, children are no longer themselves and under this disguise can play out their own guilt, anxiety and fears. In a story they hear how other children deal with these problems; in dressing-up play they do it themselves. One feature of dressing-up play in which we can see a child's personal fears being expressed is revealed in a child frightening other children. What he is probably unconsciously doing is throwing onto other children his own fear of being frightened by imaginary monsters and fierce lions that live on staircases and dark corners. And it is very likely that, by playing in this way in a situation where, as in story play, everything is apparently under control, he is coming to terms with his own fear. He is 'sublimating' or channelling his emotions and eventually making fear meaningful rather than chaotic and irrational. For fear properly channelled serves a useful purpose as a means of defence against danger and the unknown, as we have already observed. Play includes not only adventure and risk but also rational fear.

A play sequence with a child wearing a hat or dress or some other form of total disguise is rather like an acted story in which we shift the blame from ourselves to someone else. So the child says, in effect: 'I'm not doing this. It's the cat'. Or, to go back to Maurice Sendak's story, it is not Max who is responsible for mischief, but the wolf-suit! This aspect of play is seen in a variation of dressing-up play, in which children dress up teddies and dolls who are then described as 'naughty' and in need of punishment. Teddies and dolls are not only the objects of a child's love, but also the scapegoats of their world. We shall return to this aspect of play in Chapter 7 when discussing toys.

A fourth purpose of dressing-up play is the way it reflects occupational roles like nurses, busmen, train drivers, dentists, doctors, spacemen, as well as the familiar mothers and fathers. Occasionally, you meet people who say that by allowing children to play certain roles, especially the traditional sex roles of mother and father, indoctrination takes place. There is no doubt that the home influences a great deal of what children do. For example, a home where mother and father read a lot will affect a child's attitude towards books. A four-year-old whose grandfather was a builder and decorator continually played at painting houses, though whether he will eventually become a builder like his grandfather remains to be seen. Another four-year-old whose father was a doctor, drew and painted 'lungs', no doubt because he had seen pictures in his father's books.

Personally, I do not see how anyone can avoid influencing children in some way. We have all become very sensitive about this, and maybe we ought to try to influence them in certain ways a little more than we do! One possible answer to the charge of 'indoctrination' or unnecessary influence is to encourage children to experiment with many roles and it is in this respect that education for under-fives has much to offer.

Practical hints

In practical terms, to encourage dressing up and role-play whether in home, playgroup, nursery or first school, we need to supply children with as wide a range of old clothes and hats as possible. Curtains, table-cloths, sheets and shawls, in fact anything that children can drape around themselves, are useful basic materials.

Children also need special items like cowboy trousers, Red Indian suits and head-dresses, nurses' uniforms, aprons, long dresses, doctor's white coats and stethoscope, pairs of old shoes. They love the feel and sound of grown-up shoes slipping and slapping along the floor as they shuffle round in imitation of the adult world. And hats of all kinds, shapes and sizes are essential for reasons we have discussed. Moreover, the more like life, the more real they are, the better.

All this material can be kept in a box, suitcase or old trunk. Ideally, this should be easily accessible to a child in the home or to the children in a playgroup situation. They should be able to take out what they want when they want it. Little more encouragement than making the material available is needed, though parents and teachers can join in the dressing up by accepting the roles the children are playing and talking to them about them. Never laugh at what the children are doing. To them it is serious and absorbing though it may be extremely funny to the adult watching. Children easily accept the new role another child is playing. For example, I remember seeing one four-year-old boy dressed in a rabbit suit being fed on beads, which they said were his lettuces!

The value of role-play, of which dressing up is an integral part, cannot be overestimated. It has sound psychological and sociological foundations in that all kinds of anxiety neuroses might be avoided under the guise of another *persona*. And as a means of learning to live in society, the importance of role-play is always being stressed by sociologists. It is important because it helps children to experiment with different ways of life and eventually to discover their own selfhood.

7 Toy play

Every child needs toys, though seldom of the expensive kind that manufacturers sometimes persuade parents and relations to buy. There is little doubt that choosing toys for children can be a problem and buying them a costly business. But if we know something about how and why children play with toys, it might help us choose those toys which will not only arouse and maintain interest, but also provide genuine learning situations.

Now if this sounds as if toys should be chosen for their educative value, we have to remember that for a child, all play is learning, and that toy play is only a particular kind of learning. Watch an under-five furiously filling a bucket with earth, sand or stones, or frantically digging in the ground—totally absorbed in what he is doing—and you get some idea of what play means. It is, in fact, indistinguishable from work. And effective toys are 'work things' for play, or 'play things' for work, whichever you prefer. This leads me to suggest a definition of a toy.

What is a toy?

We can define a toy as a 'plaything' or better still, as 'a thing for play'. This may be a rather broad definition, but it does mean that we can include such things as climbing frames and wendy houses as well as the more obvious types of toys like building bricks, engines and dolls' houses. It is, of course, possible to put toys into categories according to their size, but it is more relevant to discuss them in terms of the way they are actually used by children. Thus a climbing frame does not serve precisely the same purpose as a building brick. Yet there are common factors in every form of playing with toys.

The first of these factors concerns *how* a toy is used; the second, *what* the toy is being used for. For a description of how a toy is used, we need to go back to an earlier chapter when we were discussing types of play in general and using Peter Slade's terms 'personal and projected play'. And whereas role-play and dressing up, for instance, are mainly concerned with the former, toy play is an aspect of the latter.

A toy, then, is an object for 'projected play'. It is a *thing*, irrespective of its size, onto which or into which a child can project his consciousness. In his imagination, he creates new uses for the object which he then invests with a life of its own. Sometimes objects of this kind are called 'treasures' to which a child for some personal and private reason attaches a special value. A treasure may be a sea shell, an old button, a piece of wood, a tiny piece of paper, a cardboard box, a special teddy bear with an eye missing, or a chocolate wrapping. Whether it is large or small makes little difference to the value of the object as a treasure and as a source of toy play. I suppose it might be said that all these treasures, which are little more than junk to an adult, cannot properly be called toys, but according to my definition, I believe they can. So I use the word 'toy' to describe any *things* which a child imaginatively transfers from the real world to his own world of fantasy.

Fantasy is the second common factor in all forms of playing with toys and it concerns the purpose for which a toy is used. Regardless of the size of a toy, whether for example it can be held in the hand and manipulated with the fingers or not, its function is to act as a kind of key to the whole world of fantasy play. Sometimes children will use small toys in the way the maker intended. Model cars, for instance, are actually used as cars in play sequences involving garaging and so forth. Or at other times, toys like building blocks will be used for purposes other

Glove puppets.

than that for which they were intended, and they can *become* cars, trains or even people. Similarly, large toys like climbing frames can also *become* ships, castles or anything that exists in the child's imaginative or fantasy world. On the other hand, children do not have to have toys like manufactured wendy houses, because they often arrange a group of chairs to make a 'house'. And once it exists in their play, all kinds of additions are made. Cookers and washing machines, tables and chairs, cups and saucers, real or imagined, are all likely to become part of the play sequence.

In a playgroup, of course, such pieces of large apparatus as climbing frames, wendy houses and hidey-hole boxes are usually the centre of co-operative play activities and for this reason alone, every playgroup should possess all these basic 'toys'. In the home, however, substitutes can be found. For example, chairs can be re-arranged, old cardboard containers used and a hidey-hole created under the table; and within the play world of each of these improvised toys a child may very well use smaller toys, rather like props in the theatre, to extend the imagined world even further. Manufactured toys are obviously very useful, but they are not absolutely essential to toy play, for in toy play any *thing* can literally become *any* thing.

Describing toys in this way means that we have to understand some of the more puzzling aspects of a child's use of 'things for play'. For example, how often have parents spent a great deal of money on an expensive doll which gives *them* satisfaction but only fleeting pleasure to their child? And how often does father or mother complain that their five-year-old has discarded a costly toy and is now playing with the box it came in? While the electrically operated, exact-in-every-detail, scale model racing car lies neglected in a corner, their lucky offspring is happily sailing the cardboard box to a secret island.

But the cardboard box is just as much a toy as the racing car, for the value of 'a thing for play' lies not in its cost, or the accuracy with which it copies a real-life object like car, train or doll, but the possibilities it opens up to a child for creative, imaginative play.

As parents and teachers, we do not always appreciate either the value a child places on his treasures, or why he uses a toy for a purpose other than what it was intended for, mainly because we fail to understand that the toy or treasure belongs to the child's private world of fantasy. Indeed, we might even call this world his personal mythology, since in using his treasures he is trying to explain to himself what he sees and hears around him.

Playing with toys, whatever form they take, undoubtedly helps children to develop their intellect and, in particular, their linguistic skill. A child experiments with sounds, sizes and movements making his 'toy' behave rather like a ventriloquist's dummy, and if we do a little discreet eavesdropping, we shall often hear him imitating the voice of parent, playgroup leader or teacher. The experience can be quite enlightening!

Glove and finger puppets are valuable toys because they are yet another means of enabling children to play out the fear of an actual world which is daily growing bigger and more frightening. By reducing this world to manageable proportions in the puppet or miniature world, children begin to accept it because they feel they have a measure of control over what happens in it.

The functions of toys

In the first place, as we have just seen, a toy becomes part of the child's private world of fantasy, and by playing with his treasures he begins to explain the events in the real world to his own satisfaction. Teddy bears and dolls can be sounding-boards for his speech as a child talks to them and as he pretends that they talk back to him. In this way he tries to deal with his own questions and to answer them in his own way.

So a child projects his growing awareness of the world around him on to or into the toy, testing and trying out new ways of speaking, and gradually learning how to communicate.

In the second place, toys are sometimes used as scapegoats as described earlier in the chapter on fantasy play. Over forty years ago, Susan Isaacs, one of the pioneers in understanding young children, stressed the need for adults to appreciate the acute emotional conflicts that take place in very young children. 'The child,' she wrote, 'will not be able to tell even the most sympathetic adult about his wishes and anxieties. They lie far too deep in him, beyond the reach of words . . . The guilt and dread bound up with these complex shifting feelings are indeed so strong that the child has to keep his own thoughts turned away from them. He comes to deny in himself, not only *behaving* angrily or possessively, but even *wanting* to behave so.' All forms of play can help a child to express, sublimate or channel his guilt and dread. But toys, of whatever kind, are also invaluable as objects on which the child can vent his feelings of anger and frustration, feelings which, as Susan Isaac remarks, the child himself is loath to admit to himself. And, of course, toys are often objects of affection and love, perhaps as substitutes for a temporarily absent mother or father.

Feelings of guilt and fear, Susan Isaacs has suggested, spring from a child's longing to have his mother to himself and anger at his father or the new baby whom he sees as rivals in affection. These feelings 'can in time be tempered and socialised in their ways of expression', continues Susan Isaacs, 'but, in the meantime, they and the guilt belonging to them find an outlet in roundabout ways, which we are only now beginning to understand'.

When these words were written, the educational value and function of play were only dimly appreciated and even then by a

Adjusting to the new arrival.

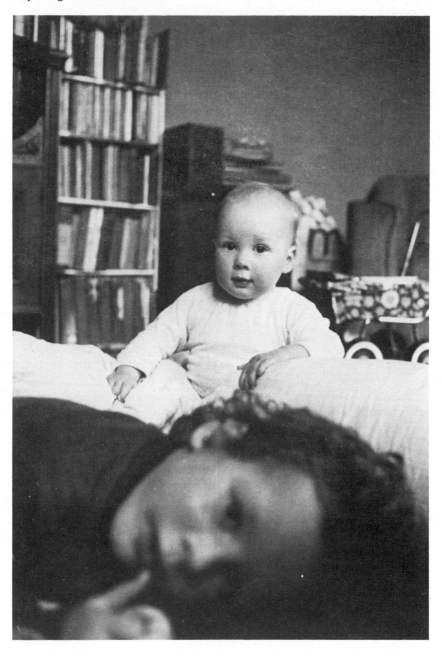

very few of what were then considered 'trendy' educators. We now know better and most educationists would accept that play in general and toy play in particular is an invaluable means of helping children resolve these emotional conflicts, and this leads us to the next major function of toys.

In the third place, then, toys can be used as substitutes for a new brother or sister and can often prepare the way for the coming baby, who may initially be regarded as a rival in the family. Though everything may be done to prevent a four-year-old from feeling displaced in family affection, he or she may not be entirely convinced. Somehow, the older child has got to accept that the new arrival will at first be the centre of affection. Playing with a toy can help in achieving this acceptance.

For example, one four-year-old, whose mother was expecting a baby, played with some other children at washing dolls. He said he was getting ready for the baby. Apart from the obvious advantages it had in showing how boys and girls can share domestic tasks and that certain activities are not specifically reserved for either girls or boys this incident revealed that the four-year-old was already beginning to accept and incorporate the new arrival into his pattern of life.

Another and sometimes very distressing use of toys, at least from the parents' point of view, is revealed in deliberate 'cruelty' on the part of the child towards a favourite doll, but this behaviour is quite normal. The child may be imaginatively substituting the doll for a baby brother or sister, who is seen as a rival for parental affection. Usually the playing out of the hatred of a rival turns into love and affection, but without opportunities for fantasy play through toys, real harm might be done. An actual example will illustrate this particular function of a toy as an instrument in emotional release.

A three-and-a-half-year-old boy continually played at drowning a small doll by pushing it under water. He said the doll was his brother who happened to be two years younger. The mother of the boys, naturally somewhat distressed, believed that one day the elder child would actually drown the younger boy. What eventually happened was that, after two years in a playgroup, the elder boy showed genuine care and affection for his little brother, whom he had originally regarded as a rival for his mother's affections.

Toys, then, can be both scapegoats and substitutes—functions they have always had since a human being first picked up a pebble or a piece of wood and pretended it was another human being to play with, to love or hate or worship.

But toys can also be used as tools in the extension of a child's physical and intellectual abilities and this leads us to a fourth function of play which relates to a particular kind of toy. This is the puzzle, fitting or matching type, that requires children to recognise, sort and fit various shapes into a pattern. For the very young, the shapes might be large, wooden cut-out animals that fit into a picture. For slightly older children there are jig-saw puzzles with the individual pieces cut into two or three large sections. Thus a child, instead of recognising the actual picture of the animal which coincides with the wooden shape, moves on to recognising the shape itself without reference to the animal's picture.

Picture puzzles and fitting games encourage manipulative skills and are especially useful both in home and playgroups as an introduction to number and letter recognition, a prerequisite for reading.

Manipulative skills can be encouraged by using pastry sets and carpentry tools—the real things, not pseudo-tools that never work! Pastry-making and pastry-cutting shapes may not be mother's idea of toy play, neither may the hammering and cutting of wood which an under-five is quite capable of doing, but it should be realised that both activities are play to the child, if we remember that young children do not distinguish between work and play and that their 'playing at work' is only using toys as tools or vice-versa!

Toys, especially of the large kind, are useful in playgroups and first schools for the encouragement of co-operative fantasy play. Home corners, either set up inside a wendy house or literally in a corner of the room with cookers, washers, ironing boards, a telephone—the real thing if the local post office engineers can be persuaded to part with an old one—will become the focus for conversation and hence, another possible therapeutic means of language development. 'Hidey-holes' too are most valuable as places where a child can be quiet and, from his point of view, out of sight for a while. Here, perhaps with a playmate or two, there exists a secret world, separated from actual space and time, a world where many of the other functions of play just described can be fulfilled.

Choosing toys

Choosing the right kind of toy is extremely important. Essentially, a toy should be intellectually flexible. By this I mean the kind of toy which encourages the imagination in a constructive way. A really effective toy will stimulate a child to create a world around it, and, by so doing, will help him gain practice in accepting and rejecting the impressions that are continually pouring into him through his senses. Subsequently, he shuffles the notions he has gained of the outside world, even generating new ones, until the picture begins to fit in with his own expanding view of the life around him. The process, as Piaget has called it, is one of 'assimilation and accommodation' of experience. Firstly, the child assimilates the new information and, secondly, accommodates or adjusts what he has previously learned in order to accept the new material. It is in the accommodating process that toys literally *play* a fundamental and necessary part. So the more intellectually flexible a toy is, the more accommodating it can become.

We should try to provide toys which can *become* any *thing,* rather than those which are unalterably what they are. A train set may be 'just what Johnny ordered', but, as we mentioned earlier, most of us have seen how Johnny plays with the box the train set came in! From my own experience and from watching young children play, I know there is very little you can do with a model train that runs on a track. Basically, there are only three possible manoeuvres: forward, reverse and stop! You soon tire of this, just as you might soon tire of a walkie-talkie doll, once it has shown off its stereo-typed vocabulary and remarkable biological simulations. On the other hand, a large wooden engine, without a track to restrict movement, can be pushed and pulled anywhere, thus meeting a young child's need for sensori-motor experience. A toy may be the toymaker's triumph, but a disaster to a child's imagination. We should not be surprised, therefore, if complicated mechanical toys soon bore a child.

In *Choosing Toys for Children,* a very practical book on the subject of toys, Sten Hegeler describes an experiment with a number of children of different ages. Two rooms were filled with toys: one with mechanically exciting things like electric and clockwork trains and cars: '. . . clockwork animals and people that hopped and ran about . . . the other room was filled with bricks and tools and boxes and planks and every conceivable kind of building set . . .' The children were allowed to choose to play in either room. For the first few days they chose the room filled with the mechanical toys and then they turned to the other room. 'For weeks on end', Hegeler comments, 'they built and constructed with just those toys that modern educationists and psychologists regard as the right ones'.

In view of these remarks, construction-type toys seem best for children. Building bricks, blocks and miniature engineering kits are excellent and there are many such kits designed for use by children of all ages. But do look at the label on the box. Nothing is more frustrating than to see pictured on the lid of the box a great bridge spanning the Amazon, which the bits and pieces in the box cannot possibly build. Good construction kits never deceive in this way.

Construction is, of course, a version of creativity and you do not have to have manufactured kits for this purpose. Boxes, cartons, cotton reels and so on, in fact any kind of junk can be used to create a toy which can then be played with. This aspect of toys is discussed in the following chapter on junk play.

But all children, despite the value of junk and the construction type of toy, naturally like manufactured toys as well, so how can we choose these toys wisely and well?

Never tell a child how a toy is to be used and never be surprised at the way he plays with it. To say: 'Do it like this!' will probably turn the child away from playing with that particular toy. It will almost certainly make him cross! On the other hand, if he asks for help, then help should be given, but always with plenty of conversation so that the experience of playing is shared between child and parent or child and teacher.

There is, of course, a definite place for toys like dolls' houses with accessible furniture, prams, cradles, ironing boards, wheelbarrows, trains and, of course, the tricycle—every under-five loves a three-wheeler! But do remember you are buying a toy to please the child—not yourself! Remember, too, that a four-year-old may be satisfied with a big wooden engine to pull along, but by the time he is six, he may prefer a smaller engine with some realistic details. And this brings us to a general point about the size of toys for handling and manipulation with the fingers.

The size of toys

The size of toys in relation to the age of a child is important. For example, it is not always a good idea to give a three-year-old a tiny model car, because he has insufficient physical skill to manipulate it satisfactorily and he will probably find it difficult to avoid stepping on it. On the other hand, a five-year-old may find great satisfaction in having something which is very like the real thing, and which is small enough to handle. A working rule is that the younger the child the bigger the toy. The older the child, the more capable he is of manipulative skills and he is therefore able to hold small objects. So for the three-year-olds, big, strong, wooden toys are best. Pull-along trucks with coloured blocks to load and unload are excellent. And if an engine is big enough to sit in or on, so much the better.

To summarise the main points about choosing toys, we can say firstly that the younger the child the bigger the toy should be. Secondly, a really effective toy is one that has the possibility of *becoming* anything, rather than one that unalterably is a particular thing. In fact, good toys should stimulate the children's imagination and, as Hegeler says, 'They do this when they set the child little tasks that he is not able to do straightaway but wants to try to do'. Building bricks and blocks and all kinds of constructional toys are excellent for both home and playgroup or nursery school. Thirdly, toys should be strong enough to withstand what to the child may be investigation, but to the adult wanton destruction. And this leads us to consider a puzzling facet of child behaviour.

Playing to destruction

We have already mentioned that children sometimes engage in what I call 'playing to destruction'. There are perhaps three possible explanations of destructive play and all need to be understood.

Firstly, the sound of collapsing bricks can cause delight in the destroyer. The child is learning that he can actually *cause* the collapse and hence the noise.

Related to this is the second possible explanation. Destruction can be a means of establishing territorial rights. In the natural world a robin sings to demonstrate that he really is cock robin in his part of the garden. Similarly, a child tries to assert himself as he feels his way into the strange new world of personal relationships. By destroying something he not only experiences being

the cause, but also shows to other people that he has made something happen. Annoying as it may be to grown-ups, the child is,
in fact, demonstrating his increasing independent powers.

Thirdly, a child can destroy merely to find out how a thing
works. He tears his Teddy apart to see whether Teddy has a
heart that beats like his own. When he fails to find one or even
to hear it beating, he begins to realise the difference between what
is alive and what is not. In fact, by destroying, a child may
actually be learning to respect life! A less obvious, though none
the less common action is the cutting of dolls' hair which sometimes distresses a parent who has brought the doll. This is clearly
not intentional destruction, but a logical step to take: if a four-
year-old has her hair cut, why should she not cut her doll's?
Anyway, hair grows again, or so the child may think, and again
there is a way of learning to distinguish between living and non-
living materials.

Nevertheless, we should never condone destruction, even
though we must try to understand it. Yet how often do adults
themselves contribute to destructive play by clearing up the
mess, as they call it, too quickly? If toys are put away or tasks
stopped too suddenly, a play structure is destroyed as certainly
as if a child had kicked over a pile of bricks. Toys swept away
into a box or cupboard without so much as a 'by-your-leave' does
not encourage children to respect anyone else's play and the
'work' they are putting into it. You cannot stop a running child
in his tracks, neither can you stop any kind of imaginative play
without some warning. Play needs time to slow down and come
to an end. If mother breaks up the play without due warning,
there is no reason to complain if her child does the same with her
tea service. In any case, to a child, a brick is more valuable. 'Do
not be amazed at "destruction",' says Peter Slade. 'Give things
that *can* be picked to pieces. Distinguish between angry bashing
and investigation. Do not be over-ready to clear up treasures
placed in odd positions.' If we have chosen the right kind of toy
for the age of the child and approach his toy play with sympathy
and understanding, we shall at least be able to meet him half way
in his wish to indulge in 'destruction'.

Conclusion

A few final points about the function of toys in a child's life may be of some help in understanding how and why every child needs some form of toy to play with.

So far I have said nothing about toy guns or the way children will inevitably use any conveniently shaped toy, like bricks and blocks, railway track and sticks as guns, or failing an actual toy, their fingers. Controversy rages over whether to allow gun play or not, but there is no doubt that we all wish such things as guns and bombs did not exist. Yet children see and hear about these things everyday and some children are continually surrounded by real guns and explosions, so it is quite impossible in our imperfect world to insulate children from what are, unfortunately, facts of life. You would have to live in isolation to exclude guns from experience and, therefore, from children's play.

Two points about the use of guns. Firstly, because children play with guns, it does not mean they will eventually become gun-men. On the contrary, playing with guns, like fighting, enables them to distinguish between really hurting and only pretending, between real life and fantasy. And secondly, playing with guns, especially in these violent times, can help children adjust and come to terms with the actual horrors they see and hear around them. Far better to *play* with toy guns than to *use* real guns later on. I played with guns and took part in tremendous battles from a very early age, but the last thing I ever want to do now is go out and shoot someone, though I must have wiped out thousands during my life of play!

In emphasising the construction-type toy, it might seem as if I implied that such things as tool sets and pastry-making sets are toys, and of course they are, even though many adults would consider them 'educational' and different in function from model cars and dolls. Anyone who has this attitude is failing to appreciate the real function of 'projected play', which depends on 'things'. And this attitude also fails to recognise that few children in the three-to-five range make a distinction between play and work.

To quote Sten Hegeler once more: 'Every development of art and science, in building, dress, and other fields of culture and civilisation is almost immediately reflected in the toys of the period.' These comments ought to serve as both guidance and warning in our choice of toys, for they make us, as adults, ask fundamental questions about the world in which we now live and which our children will one day inherit.

Some suppliers of toys

Ventureplay, 40 Monnaread Road, Multy, Plymouth PL4 7AF.

Educational Supply Association Ltd., Pinnacles, Harlow, Essex.

James Galt & Co. Ltd., Brookfield Road, Cheadle, Cheshire. (There are Galt agencies in many shops throughout Britain.)

D. A. Finnegan Ltd., 63 Buckingham Street, Aylesbury, Bucks.

Community Playthings, Darwell, Robertsbridge, Sussex TN32 5DR. (A self-supporting religious community that makes a wide range of excellent equipment and toys. Visitors are welcome.)

All these suppliers send catalogues on request.

8   Junk play

Since junk play is like playing with home-made toys, it is, in effect, an aspect of projected play, of using 'things for play'. But things that are junk to an adult may be treasure to a child, in fact, as most of us know, children collect and keep anything and everything. Sometimes it is collected for the sheer pleasure of hoarding precious items that a child feels really belong to him. At other times, children make use of the junk and rubbish they find and turn them either actually or imaginatively into all kinds of weird and wonderful things. In this sense, junk play is not only an extension of toy play, but an activity in which the toy itself is created as well as being the inspiration of the playing.

There is nothing remarkable or new in this. One day someone in central Europe picked up an old corn husk and saw in it the possibilities of making a doll. Later, with the pioneers, the idea was taken across the Atlantic to the New World, where corn husks are still made into the American version of dolls. Ever since a human being first picked up a pebble or piece of old wood, and shaped it to represent another 'thing', junk has been transformed into toys. The first point to remember, then, is that junk has the potential of becoming a treasure. The use of old tin cans, bicycle

'Painting the house' - using large items of junk.

wheels, bent metal and so on to create modern sculpture has become almost common-place these days.

By encouraging children to make use of junk, we are doing no more than capitalising on their instincts to collect and assert their personalities over the things they have collected. We saw how this process worked in the previous chapter when we were discussing building and destructive play. In junk play, a child is literally creating new forms out of what already exists and his ability to do this often verges on the miraculous. Apparently, what a child creates corresponds in some way or ways to the growing concept of something in his mind. Perhaps this concept is only half-formed, uncontrolled and vague, at least when he tries to express it in painting or making. But to him, it is a vital means of consolidating the concept through the sensori-motor play we talked about at the beginning of the book. Young children learn through doing, by first becoming the thing and then evolving concepts. Junk play can help in forming these concepts.

So if a child tells you that the conglomeration of egg boxes, silver paper, toilet rolls and tissues is a rocket, a house, a baby's pram, a farm, or a dinosaur you must accept what he tells you, for it really has become such a thing to him. Sometimes a child will start to make something and will not even know what it is. Maybe, the concept has only partially formed in his mind and he is subconsciously seeking to find a form of expression, and only as he makes the thing does that form literally 'materialise'. Thus his concept is both expressed in the thing he has made and also reinforced in the actual making of it. And though we may not recognise the thing and therefore may not immediately understand what the child is trying to express, in junk play, as in all forms of play and as in all artistic expression, he is exploring intellectual, emotional and manipulative experiences. Taken all together, these explorations can indeed be considered as an aspect of the artistic process, because art is rather like making something out of nothing, or, more accurately, of combining and transforming what we experience through our senses into new experiences as our imagination gets to work. In short, junk play helps children to think, feel and to manipulate physical materials and intellectual concepts.

It is, of course, difficult, if not impossible, to separate the three elements since they are all present in every process of exploratory play, but it might be easier to see more precisely what is happening in junk play if each of these elements is discussed separately. So, for the sake of convenience, we shall look at the intellectual, emotional and physical aspects of junk play in turn.

Intellectual aspects in junk play

Forming concepts is essential to the process of reason and thinking in the abstract, or, to put it another way, of being able to think about something other than an actual object. Playing with junk offers the possibility of creating new forms out of those which already exist. What a child does is to see with the mind's eye, as it were, those things that could exist. So a toilet roll with an egg box stuck on at one end can become an animal of some sort, a pig or a sheep perhaps, or, if the child has other ideas, a ship, rocket or a monster! The actual thing he makes is unimportant. The main consideration is that a child sees it as something, and that he should conceive it without guidance and help from parent, supervisor or teacher.

There is, of course, a great deal of argument as to how much help a child should be given with this kind of creative work, but in junk play I believe children should be allowed complete freedom in their making. If they seek guidance and help on the technical aspects of junk play, such as how to stick pieces of cardboard together and what to use to do it, then help should be given. But there should never be any direction as to what certain items of junk can make.

One aim, if aim there has to be in junk play, is to give children a range of things to transform imaginatively into other things which are the expression of their developing concepts. This is the main reason why it is difficult to discuss junk play. For as soon as we start talking about what to make, one of the primary aims has disappeared, namely, the exploration of new materials as a means of expressing concepts. In objectifying these concepts, they are reinforced intellectually and will then become part of the schemas or mental patterns against which and with which children can make further and more detailed exploration of experiences. From the intellectual point of view, then, junk play corresponds to language play and dressing-up play, but whereas in the last two forms of play, children are exploring sounds and roles respectively, in junk play they are exploring the possibilities of establishing and rearranging mental symbols in various ways. Thus, to go back to the example of the pigs and sheep, the actual objects of toilet roll and egg box are obviously what they are and children know this. But with mental or rather imaginative manipulation of these concrete objects, new symbols are created, just as sounds and words are manipulated into new sentences. In short, junk play is a language of expression through which a child communicates both with himself, thus reinforcing the half-formed concepts and symbols in his mind, and with the outside world when he shows other people what he has made. And in this respect, puppets are invaluable.

Puppets can be made from all kinds of junk. For example, puppets from paper bags of all sizes, with eyes and mouth boldly marked on them with a felt-tipped pen, are easily and quickly made. A hole in the bag through which a finger can be poked to form a 'wiggly' nose adds to the fun! Individual-size cornflake packets with or without a stick to hold them are also useful puppets. In fact, children will create puppets as sounding-boards and scapegoats for their own thoughts and feelings out of practically anything. And the perennial fascination of Punch and Judy testifies to the power of puppets to delight and hold the interest of young children—and old!

With puppets there is a double delight; there is fun in making them and fun in using them. Puppets, then, show very clearly that, in junk play, the process of making and the product of the making are both important. To put the matter in the more technical terms of educational philosophy, the value of junk play is both intrinsic and extrinsic. The process, however, is much more important and significant than the product especially with regard to a child's intellectual development.

Emotional aspects of junk play

An important function of junk play is to help a child channel and control his emotions. All of us experience days when everything seems to go wrong. The children annoy us and the milkman forgets to leave the milk and the toast gets burnt and the car fails to start and on top of everything it rains! The day begins in annoyance and frustration, and many adults have their own personal safety-valves that enable them to let off emotional steam. Mother makes some pastry and as she pummels and kneads the dough, she is working out her own frustrations. And who knows, subconsciously the dough might be the source of the frustration, though instead of punching the milkman, hitting the children and kicking the car, she pummels the dough in what is, in effect, a constructive operation. She *makes* something out of her frustration and bad temper. Children need the same kind of outlet, a channel and control for their annoyance and we shall return to the use of pastry, clay and similar materials in the next chapter, but junk play can function in the same kind of way as play with materials like clay, water and sand.

For example, cutting cardboard and paper, screwing up old tissues, snipping pieces of wool and string, then dipping all these bits and pieces in paste and glue and sticking them together lets children vent their feelings in a controlled and constructive way. In addition, of course, there is the intellectual value of actually making something which we discussed just now.

Apart from channelling frustrations and anger in junk play, children can overcome a lack of confidence in themselves. For

Concentrating on manipulative skills.

example, some children, perhaps as a result of having over-anxious, over-protective parents who have not allowed their children to take reasonable risks in their play, are afraid to trust themselves in cutting and sticking. Lack of confidence in trying out new ideas, in exploring their physical potential in running, jumping and climbing and so on, is often reflected in an apparent inability to create new forms in art. More importantly, it may be reflected in the slow learner. Taking a physical risk is similar in motive though not in scale, of course, to taking a risk by cutting a shape from a piece of old cardboard, or even trying to master the techniques of reading.

If then, we can encourage children to take these creative risks, by cutting boldly, painting with flourish and flair and getting messy with paste, we shall, perhaps, be giving a child the necessary confidence he needs in the really big risks he has to take in life itself. And I mention 'getting messy', because, again, the over-protected child is frequently somewhat fastidious and afraid to get dirty. But life is neither clean nor protected and in a very simple way, junk play contributes to a child's great need for confidence in himself, his ideas, emotions and physical potential.

Physical aspects of junk play

There is not a great deal to say about this aspect of junk play. Clearly enough, one of the major uses of junk play is the opportunity it offers for children to test their manipulative skills. Cutting with scissors that really cut, twisting pieces of paper into shapes and trying to thread pieces of wool and string through holes pushed with a pencil through paper and card are all manoeuvres that demand considerable skill from an under-five. But the concentration under-fives show in attempting difficult tasks and persevering with them indicates how well they can work given the chance. But chance they must have, the chance to make a mess, to make something that is apparently meaningless to an adult, the chance to destroy, to recreate in new forms, for this is the essence of all creative enterprises whether as a fully fledged artist or as a curious, frustrated under-five.

Practical aspects of junk play

For reasons already given, I do not intend to describe what to do in junk play; in any case all we need is a supply of junk! The children will do the rest, providing we give them the encouragement and confidence to experiment with it.

So, even if the home becomes cluttered with bits and pieces of this and that, or even if the playgroup or first school is encumbered with the rubbish of many homes, parents, supervisors and teachers should be scavengers, collecting all kinds of apparently useless materials. It is said that our civilisation is populated by wastemakers, and in America it is claimed that 18 tons of garbage are produced by every individual each year. If we can make use of a tiny fraction of what we throw away by giving it to children to create and construct with, maybe we shall see that everything has its uses.

Every home, playgroup, nursery or first school should have a box or bag of odds and ends picked up by parent or teacher or children. It should include such items as old Christmas and birthday cards for cutting up into patterns or pictures, string, wool, egg boxes, sea shells, matchboxes, plastic bottles, cotton reels, milk tops, cheese boxes, offcuts of soft wood, toilet rolls, coloured sweet papers and so on. Tissues and newspaper are also good for squashing up into different shapes. Paper clips to bend and twist, elastic bands, paste and glue are all useful means of fixing the oddments together. Junk play can produce two-dimensional and three-dimensional objects.

Two-dimensional junk play is really another name for making a collage. All you need for a collage is a sheet of paper or card and heaps of oddments like those I have just listed. A child will select pieces of cloth, paper, string and so on and stick them on to the paper with paste or glue. Sometimes the result will be recognisable. At other times we shall have no idea what the collage represents, but this matters not at all. The materials, their texture and colour, are being explored and the ideas are already being shifted around in the child's mind. He may, of course, wish to tell you about the collage. If so, then by all means let him, but never rush him into explaining his work. Once he has finished it, he will probably lose interest. He might say: 'I can't do any more' or 'I've done it now!' And no amount of prodding and persuading will make him pick up the work and start again.

Three-dimensional or solid junk play consists in using the items noted previously. Children might use a box instead of a sheet of paper as a starting point and then literally build up the thing from solid junk of the matchbox/toilet roll type. Glue rather than paste will probably be necessary in solid junk play, since a stronger adhesive will be required to hold the contraption together. Nothing is more frustrating than to have a limp and soggy thing soaked in a paste that sticks nothing!

All that has been said about two-dimensional junk play applies here. Give help and guidance when and where a child needs it; confidence in relationships is gained when a child freely asks for help. We should rather worry about the child who sits sobbing quietly because he cannot manage something. And there are still a few of these children around in our schools! Home and play-group can both help to satisfy a child's need for encouragement and confidence in his own abilities and in his relationships with grown-ups.

And finally in discussing aspects of junk play it must be stressed that we should never tell children what to do. The trouble with books and articles on the subject is that the writers try to give guidance knowing only too well that they should not be giving anyone any guidance at all! So, do let the children really explore the materials in their own way and even if the result does appear a meaningless mass of paper and string, always praise it. The process itself may have achieved something invaluable in relieving frustration and the gaining of confidence and the reinforcement of symbolic thinking.

9 Playing with natural materials

In certain respects, natural materials are a form of junk. But they have particular properties and can be used for special purposes. Playing with natural materials can fulfil all the functions of junk play with the addition of a few others that manufactured junk cannot.

Natural play materials are all around us. Natural materials belong to our environment, and therefore they offer different opportunities for play depending on their nature. For example, I remember talking to teachers in Jamaica about the potential uses of the huge seedpods of the flamboyant or poinciana tree. The teachers suddenly remembered the many different ways in which they had used these pods when they were children, but which they had long since forgotten. The pods are black, about a foot long and ridged inside like a gigantic pea pod. 'We used to count the steps inside', said one teacher. 'It's like a ladder', said another. 'We put one seed inside and used it as a shaker', said a Barbadian.

I give this example to show how people have been using natural materials for play for years, just like the corn husk doll of central Europe and the United States I mentioned earlier. So, apart from the possibilities for creative work common to junk play and all artistic activities, playing with natural materials makes us look at the world around us. It makes us more aware of the variations in the shape and colour of rocks and stones, wood, twigs and leaves. It can make us more sensitive to the feel of natural objects, the texture of tree barks, the difference between wet and dry sand and the sensation of water itself. And the basic materials for art have always been those taken from nature! The paint for the ancient cave paintings was made from powdered rocks that produced the red and brown ochre colourings, whilst the 'canvas' was the rock itself! We need to become much more aware of our environment, its beauty and its value; natural materials are treasures in their own right and few children, given the chance and a gentle nudge now and then, will fail to see the attraction in the shapes and textures of leaves and stones, and to be fascinated by the colour and the roundness of pebbles worn smooth by the action of sea and sand. Moreover, through using certain natural materials, water and sand, for example, a child's growing awareness of his own powers to cause events to happen (which, you may remember, was a possible reason for destructive play), is immediately sharpened. He can see the results of his actions at once.

And at this point it is worth quoting Susanna Miller on the implications of sand and water play. 'Once the child becomes capable of appreciating the effects of his own actions on different materials trying these out seems to follow automatically, limited only by his skill and the nature of the material. Splashing in water, pouring it out, running sand through one's hands, or displacing it from one heap to another, do not make great demands on skill, but do produce immediate and continued ripples and visible changes. Not surprisingly, sand and water play are the earliest nursery favourites.' We can discuss the value of play with natural materials under the same headings, of intellectual and emotional aspects, as applied to junk play, though it will not be necessary to repeat the comments on its usefulness in the development of manipulative skills, since the points made then are equally relevant here. Once again, we must stress that emotional and intellectual developments are complementary and cannot really be separated. For convenience, however, we can look at each in turn beginning with the use of natural materials in helping children to understand, channel and control their emotions.

Emotional development and natural materials

In discussing junk play, we dealt with its relationship to intellectual development first, but here I have reversed the order, because it seems to me that, whereas junk play primarily furthers intellectual development, playing with natural materials is mainly concerned with the emotions. But this is purely a matter of opinion, and, as I said just now, you cannot really separate the intellect and the emotions from learning situations in practice.

We shall deal with various forms of natural materials in turn, grading each according to its texture.

Water

Water is soothing. Watching water, just as much as playing with it, can give a sense of peace and quietness. Not always, of course, as everyone who has ever splashed in puddles and thrown water over someone knows very well!

Part of the soothing effect of water may derive from its being a substitute for the temporary comfort we experienced as babies when filling a nappy. Momentarily, there is warmth, which quickly changes to discomfort it is true, but the ephemeral comfort is remembered and it may be that if we want psychological explanations for the delight in water play, this is the most likely.

Contrary to what I have heard some playgroup supervisors claim, water play does not stimulate 'toilet trotting' or 'wetting pants'. As children discover their control over the splashing and trickling of water through their fingers and hands, so by a process of substitution it can also give a measure of control over urination. Water play is worth trying with a habitual 'bed-wetter', providing, of course, that there are no other obvious causes for the bed-wetting such as anxiety and lack of parental security. Many children fear wetting themselves, and water play, which they find manageable, may help them to manage their own 'waterworks'.

We noted in a previous chapter the case of a little boy who continually tried to drown a doll because he was jealous of his baby brother, and it is worth repeating here the value of water play as an aspect of therapeutic fantasy play. A child is angry with his friend or his pet animal or just himself and he takes it out of a toy duck or doll which he thrashes about in the water. Water, too, symbolically washes the guilt away. Children can

Water play.

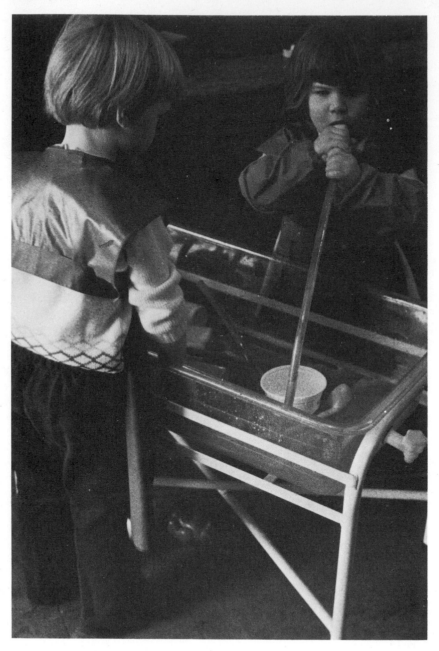

find great comfort in water when they feel guilty about the mess or mischief they have made. If we find water play in the home something to be avoided on account of possible consequences, a bowl of water in the garden, in the backyard, or in the garage will be enough. Failing that, the use of wash basin, bath or sink for a short time will work marvels. So, never underestimate the value of water play and its effect on the emotional development of children.

Sand

Closely related to water is sand. Sand is a basic natural material for play. Like water it can be moved around but never destroyed. Its shape, like water, is continually changing yet it remains miraculously the same! A child can perhaps gain a feeling of authority over the shapes formed from the material together with an underlying sense of permanence, because the material itself is indestructible. It can be dug, shaken, stamped on—if there is enough of it—and yet somehow it comes out the same every time. Sometimes on Christmas Day I walk along the seashore and always have my secret beliefs confirmed that children often prefer playing with nature to playing with expensive toys. For there they are, the under-fives—and the not so young too!— digging furiously in the sand with battered spades and buckets.

Sand for play should be both wet and dry. Dry sand can be trickled through the fingers rather like water whereas wet sand can be moulded and shaped this way and that. Castles and sand pies, birthday cakes and channel tunnels all emerge from wet sand. And like water, there is a possible substitution for a baby's fascination with, and temporary comfort in anal excrement in dabbling the fingers in sand.

Clay and pastry

Clay is similar to sand in its effects, but, of course, is even firmer and has greater potential for making something more permanent. With clay, too, you can work out aggression in a material that requires more control than either sand or water. Playing with clay, like plasticine or pastry, which are not strictly 'natural materials' at all but can be considered as serving similar purposes to clay, enables a child to demonstrate his complete mastery over form.

Pastry is a useful material because for young children in particular it is slightly easier to handle than clay. Often a piece of pastry in the hand of a child acts as some sort of solace. Maybe it works in the same way as worry beads do for adults; whatever the explanation, holding on to something that can be pressed and squashed and manipulated certainly provides comfort.

Wood

Many mothers and teachers express alarm at the thought of under-fives playing with tools. But I must stress that they should be given *real* tools and not the ineffective type you can buy in 'tool sets' which are frustrating because the saw cuts nothing!

The texture of wood needs to be felt. For example, the difference between planed and unplaned wood should be experienced and both compared with the wood on a tree trunk. A pile of nails, a hammer and some pieces of soft wood offer endless opportunities for hammering out aggression and frustration in a constructive way.

Quite possibly, the result of the carpentry will not be apparent to the adult, but the process is exciting if nothing else. For one thing, a child can control the noise of hammering, and here again we have the delight of a child in being a cause, for he or she is master of it. And I say 'she' because girls can get just as much pleasure out of hammering, sawing and drilling as boys. In the same way, boys need to work with pastry.

Rocks and stones

Stones and rocks vary in shape and colour. Some are sharp and some are smooth and round so that they provide excellent opportunities for children to feel their textures and to take note of their colours. One four-year-old boy held a small white stone he had been given throughout a whole morning. Presumably, he felt a sense of security in handling and actually owning the pebble. It was his and it felt good!

In all these examples of natural materials, and there must be many more, there are infinite possibilities to explore textures, colours and, with some of the larger sea shells, the curious sound of the sea that seems to be locked up in their crevices. So the potential for emotional development is only a part of the value that playing with natural materials can offer, and the working out of aggression, frustration, guilt and so on is linked with the

Pastry.

Carpentry.

sheer pleasure in handling and making something, and in holding and owning things that belong to the earth and sea. But encouraging children's awareness of the environment overlaps with and is really bound up with the use of natural materials in intellectual development.

Intellectual development and natural materials

Again it will be convenient to look at each of the natural materials in turn to see what specific function it serves.

Water

Water play can give a child the experience of shape, size and volume as he pours from one cup to another. Filling plastic bottles from another container may not seem to be achieving very much, but it is giving a child some idea of how much liquid goes into or over a cup.

For water play any containers are useful. Plastic detergent bottles, some with holes bored in them, a piece of plastic tube, a cork, a ping-pong ball, a tea strainer, a rubber glove or a boat a child has made in woodwork are all necessary for really effective water play. I remember watching a five-year-old girl playing with a rubber glove for a long time. She filled the fingers with water from a jug, emptied the water, refilled individual fingers, tried to sink the glove when empty, then when full and so on. In fact, by doing this with a rubber glove or with bottles, corks, wood or whatever, children are learning the difference between sinkable and non-sinkable objects. Straws can be used to blow ping-pong balls along the surface of the water and the sheer joy of blowing bubbles is universal. In water play, the concepts of weight, density and volume are being very slowly constructed, though the mastery of such concepts will not come till later in a child's life, probably not until he has reached the age of six or seven.

Sand

Containers are also useful for playing with sand. Sieves, too, are necessary in order that children can explore the relationship of sizes. For example, stones will not go through the holes in the sieve, but sand will. This may seem obvious to us as adults, but it is not at all obvious to a four-year-old who has to explore and experience the difference. A simple pair of scales made from two pieces of wood, one upright and the cross beam hinged on a hook, allows children to compare weights. For instance, they can try comparing the weights of wet sand and dry sand. The first tentative lesson in mathematics is already taking place!

Clay

Apart from the emotional release gained through playing with clay, actually making something, a small pot for instance, is an ideal way of encouraging physical manipulation. Discovering the contrast between trying to make a pot with wet sand, which will not stay for long where it is put, and using clay, plasticine or pastry can lead to an appreciation of the different properties of materials. Sometimes, of course, a child will just go on moulding a piece of clay without any obvious results except the built-in pleasure obtained from the moulding. One rising five when asked by another child what she had made replied: 'It can be anything!' In fact, she had made a very accurate model of a tortoise! Patterns can be made on the clay with a piece of wood or matchsticks.

Pastry

We commented earlier that pastry could be more easily worked than clay because it is more pliable. It can be rolled into worms— which children love to do—punched with holes and cut into shapes. A supply of pastry cutters like geometrical shapes, or patterns like gingerbread men, will add to the pleasure obtained from controlling the material. But sometimes let a child make a shape with his hands rather than with the cutters. And if on special occasions the result of all the rolling and cutting and shaping can actually be cooked, we shall be showing what happens when heat is applied. The pastry becomes hard and, if someone can be persuaded to fire the little clay pots, the children can see how cups and saucers and plates are made.

Wood

Soft wood offcuts which are fairly easy to saw and which take nails without too much physical effort are ideal for constructing all kinds of things. Aeroplanes are common constructions because you only need two basic strips of wood to represent the fuselage and the wings. I once watched a four-year-old girl hammering four nails into a square piece of wood. She was merely experimenting with the hammering, but when the nails were firmly in place—without help, I should add—she wound coloured wool round and round and in and out making a criss-cross pattern. Then the wool came off and she turned the wood with its four nails upside down and claimed she had made a table. And, of course, she had!

Clearly, this form of play is closely akin to junk play. The difference, if difference there is, may be in the quality of the materials used and the range of tools provided, most of which require a greater degree of manipulative skill. Nevertheless, playing with natural materials, junk play and the various art activities we shall discuss in the next chapter, are all aspects of 'projected play' and help to develop the emotional, intellectual and physical elements in a child's growing personality.

10   Art and play

In this chapter, I have no intention of discussing the meaning of art or theories as to its origin. Neither do I intend to give detailed practical hints on what to do in art for under-fives. In any case, there are many excellent books dealing with all these topics. What I want to look at is the connection between art and play and the specific contribution that art can and does make to the learning and living of young children.

No doubt some art critics and educationists, particularly those concerned with art in education, will disagree with my separation of junk and natural materials from what, for want of a better phrase, I can only describe as the more 'traditional' art forms. And I admit that, as I pointed out in the chapter on junk play, natural materials have always constituted a basis for art. Collage, for example, using the natural and manufactured 'rubbish' of the environment, is well-established as a legitimate, now almost traditional art form. It is in the use of materials from the environment that the world of adult art is linked with the art of children. Moreover, an interest in children's art has influenced many modern artists because its naivety and simplicity are claimed to reflect a primitive kind of innocence.

In other words, so the argument runs, when man was in his childhood at the dawn of time, there was a simplicity and truthfulness, a sincerity and perception, which civilisation has blurred if not entirely blotted out. Hence, along with an interest both in the use of various materials and in children's art forms, there is also an interest in primitive art, the masks and figures of Africa, the carvings of South America and the cave paintings of Europe. And in children's work and that of primitive societies two elements seem to be present, both of which indicate reasons for encouraging children to paint, draw, construct and engage in all kinds of creative activities.

These two elements can be called formal or symbolic and representational or concrete. In the first element, there is delight in exploring materials and constructing things, as in junk play. If we ask a child what he has made, most probably he will be unable to answer because he has no idea. The question is probably meaningless anyway. The delight is in the process. But in the second element there is a conscious attempt to represent something from the real world. The form of the structure or painting is *like* the thing in life. Admittedly, this is to over-simplify the whole business of art, but it may help us to see what it is we are trying to do when we give children the opportunities to experiment with various art forms.

A child's painting may be expressing those concepts we discussed earlier which have not yet properly formed in the child's mind. Or it may express nothing more than the pleasure derived from playing with materials, textures and colours. The process is of value in itself. The product has value only insofar as the child gives it value. More often than not, once a painting is done, the child has no longer any interest in it. Though at other times, especially if he is in a playgroup or school, he may want to take it home as a gift to his parents. Occasionally, a child will want to paint for a supervisor or teacher. It is his way of expressing love, and the value here lies not only in the process of the painting but in the act of giving. And in expressing his love, he is trying to communicate with the world outside him, to give something of himself, an act which corresponds to the way we give something of ourselves every time we speak.

In summarising the general approach to art for under-fives, it is helpful to quote Kenneth Jameson, whose appreciation of children's art and his writing on the subject are most perceptive and show a particular insight into the whole question of young children's art and its meaning. 'If we accept that art for the child is a language, a means of expression and communication, then logically there can be only *one* way of assessment, and that is to assess the content of the work'.

Jameson continues by drawing attention to the need for all of those concerned with young children, whether at home, in a playgroup or school, to recognise that every young child has his own personal means of expression, his own private mythology by which he is trying to interpret the world to himself. Judgement of child art cannot be made against adult standards; a very different set of criteria is involved in child art, the main aspect of which, for an under-five, is that art is play, serious and essential, but exploratory play in which the process of doing is more important—and more significant—than the product which may appear utterly meaningless to the adult.

To quote Kenneth Jameson again: 'We must always be on our guard against imposing adult standards and criteria upon him, "The arms are too short" has no place in the classroom. Such criticisms should never enter the teacher's mind, much less cross her lips.' Art for a young child is another means of exercising the instinct to play, to explore, to experience, to extend himself into the world around him. By translating what he sees and hears and feels into visual form, he is gradually making those experiences part of himself. Art is a vital means of learning. It is not an extra, but a fundamental part of an under-five's life.

In some respects all art is play. In fact, one of the main theories about the origins of art suggests that art is the result of surplus energy. When we no longer have to spend all our time making pots to cook in, there is time to spare, time to decorate the pots and make things which are not absolutely necessary for existence. This theory, though once considered sound, did not take into sufficient account the seriousness of play nor the fundamental importance of play as a means of learning both for children and adults. Play was once considered an activity of leisure, something you did when work was over but, as we discussed in Chapter 2, that is not how children regard it at all, nor is it sound psychology. Hence art is much more than a pastime, an occupation to fill up the leisure hours. And for children, and adults, too, if they would give it half a chance, art can fulfil the functions of all play activities in general, and in particular, rather more specific functions than those fulfilled by junk play and playing with natural materials which we discussed in the last two chapters.

In considering art for young children, then, I am going to define art according to the materials used. So drawing, painting, crayoning, cutting out, weaving and the use of felt pens are included in the definition, which I realise is an arbitrary one, adopted for convenience.

In a playgroup or school situation children ought to be allowed to paint whenever they wish, but in the home, of course, this may not be possible. Preparations have to be made, such as setting up the easel, putting on the apron—which all children should wear—mixing paints and so on. Nevertheless, if it is at all possible, a child should be allowed to paint at home, and to paint in a large, bold way. I vividly remember trying to paint with an inadequate painting set, whose tiny palettes were almost useless for producing thick colour. Moreover, the painting book, which provided interminable farm and zoo animals for colouring, must have done fearful damage to my creative ability in painting. And, I must admit I still find it difficult to paint, though I do sometimes try. Somewhere along the line, the free use of thick, bold colour on large sheets of paper was blocked for me.

From my own experiences several points about children's painting emerge. Firstly, paints should have a consistency that enables a large area to be covered, and covered fairly quickly. Secondly, for a small child the brushes should be fairly big; and thirdly, the paper should also be big, encouraging the wide sweeps of brush and colour which are helping a child to express the rhythm of circle and line. Later, these rhythms will be unconsciously used in his learning to write, but this is quite incidental. More important is the fact that by shaping his symbols in paint he is finding another way to express his concepts and, as in other forms of play, reinforcing them through sensori-motor learning. Large brushes on large paper offer the opportunity to make large movements in the course of objectifying half-formed concepts. In this kind of art, symbolic form may be more obvious and the child will probably not be aware of what he has actually painted. Do not ask him: 'What is that?' though you can encourage him to tell you about the painting. Even then, never push a child too hard, since you will be forcing an image onto the painting which may not have been in the child's conscious or subconscious thinking. And we want him to extend his ability for abstract

Painting.

'Making a mess'.

thought and the formation of concepts in painting play. This leads us to consider what painting does for a child.

Painting and the child

The first thing to remember is that painting is another way of expressing feelings and ideas just like all the other forms of play we have discussed. It is also a means of having fun and quite often there will be no other obvious result of painting than the pleasure a child derives from it. Thus, if it can be arranged either in the home or the playgroup or school for children to paint *when* they want to, so much the better. They are then learning to exercise their freedom of choice, to make those little decisions which are part of the process of life itself, and which provide another means of penetration into the ways of the world.

And what children find in that world will be reflected in their painting. A child takes from his environment what he sees, hears and feels. If his life is rich with experiences of all kinds, if, to put it briefly, the child is highly stimulated, then as a rule he will produce quite remarkable paintings. The most significant exceptions to this rule are those children who choose not to express themselves. Such children may play quietly in a corner by themselves where creative play itself is a form of personal art. But if a child is shy or not ready—and few three-year-olds *are* ready for co-operative, communicative play—he may wish to keep himself to himself. The only child will often find it difficult to make contact with people and if painting can be encouraged then he may gain the self-confidence he needs.

Painting of a special kind may help a child to gain confidence, because he can get dirty in a controlled and properly directed way. This is where *finger painting* is of such value. Getting the fingers well and truly mixed up in the thick paint is enjoyable at a purely sensuous level as the child stirs and feels the texture of stickiness. And then, as he moves his fingers and hands over the paper and patterns emerge, he is translating all his feelings of frustration and anxiety into visible shapes and lines and colours. He is, indeed, making contact with the world through the media of paint and paper.

Finger painting is immediate and direct, a vital means of helping the over-anxious child literally to *feel* his way into the world. Variations of finger painting are possible by using other

Finger painting.

instruments for painting. A brush is really the extension of the fingers, so why use only brushes? Try using a piece of sponge, a length of string, a comb, in fact anything which, when dipped in paint, can produce patterns of different kinds. In doing this type of painting, children are learning about the different textures of materials in addition to finding new and exciting ways of expressing their feelings and ideas.

A third point, and a very important one at that, is that painting is an outlet for a child's growing appreciation of situations and events in his widening world. Gradually his paintings become more fluent in the sense that they may tell an obvious story, or if they do not, then an under-five will often talk freely to an adult about what he has painted, relating verbally what he expressed in his own visual terms. And so he tells you a story about his painting. 'Here is a man. Now he is chopping a tree down. And he is putting the wood on the lorry. Now the lorry drives off.' In this process we have a further instance of the way in which a child moves from his isolated bits of pretence to connected sequences in his play, whether language, dressing up, story play or painting. Gradually, the child is discovering how to form concepts and connect them logically.

Do we teach painting?

The simple answer to this is 'Never', at least not to the under-five. We do not teach children how to paint for we are not trying to produce artists. On the other hand, we can encourage children to paint by developing their awareness of the world around them, its sights, sounds and texture and so on.

We should never show a child *how* to draw or paint a house, a man, a car or whatever. Direction and guidance are subtly given in the form of stimulating experiences in the home, the school and in the child's world as a whole. As ideas about what their senses tell them are provoked, children respond in certain ways and eventually express this response in their chosen play form. It may be painting, it may be dressing up or it may be in the language of stories, but it is their way of coming to terms with the world. So interference means stopping an expression, blocking the formation of thoughts and the expression of feelings and therefore a slowing up of the whole learning process. Moreover, telling a child that his painting lacks something, for example, that his picture of a man has no arms or legs is like saying that you know better than he does. His confidence suffers a setback by your remarks. After all, it is *his* painting, not yours, so do respect it.

Other means of expression in art

So far I have discussed painting and the use of brushes, fingers and other articles for putting paint on. But there are many other ways of 'making a mark', and it will be useful to note just a few.

Straightforward drawing should be done with soft pencils because the lines come out thick and dark. Also there is a likelihood of children pushing the sharp point of a hard pencil through the paper. Young children are not always aware of the pressure needed in applying pencil to paper and often tend to overdo it! There are excellent pencils on the market which are big enough for the under-five to hold. The same thing applies to paint brushes and to crayons. Always try to give children thick, stubby and short pencils, crayons and chalks.

Let children use crayons and chalks to experiment with rubbings of bark, leaves, doilies, in fact anything which will give a print when the surface is covered with a sheet of paper and the crayon, chalk or pencil is rubbed over it. Children get a tremendous thrill as they see patterns miraculously appearing. It is a kind of magic and, moreover, the child has done it and to all intents and purposes he is in control of the magic.

Heel ball, once used by shoe repairers and still obtainable, is also a useful material for making rubbings. It can now be obtained in a range of colours, including bronze and gold as well as black.

Rubbings of various surfaces give children the actual feel of textures as they move their hands in rhythmic movements across the surface. Thus, incidentally, they are learning a measure of physical skill as they manipulate the pencil, chalk or crayon.

Tracing a picture also seems like magic to a child, but there are various conflicting opinions as to the value of tracing. Some experts claim that it destroys the natural creativity of the child by restricting the freedom of his hand movements and hence his experimentation with line and direction. Others see no particular harm in tracing. I remember the pleasure in achievement I had from tracing pictures. But tracing should only be done sparingly and as an addition to not a substitute for the free painting and drawing which are the truly vital and worthwhile activities.

Tracing round shapes comes into this category too. Again there are conflicting opinions about its educational value. But as with tracing a picture, a child obtains considerable satisfaction from following the outline of a dog, cat or camel. On the other hand, there are many educationists who claim that a child should explore the shape of camel, cat or dog on his own and not be guided or restricted by what is already there. I have no definite answer. Both opinions seem to me to have sense, and as an easy way out I would advise using the shapes sparingly. They seem to fulfil the necessary sensori-motor function in the learning process of very young children. As children move their pencils round the shape they are actually feeling their way into the concept the shape symbolises. And if the child wants to cut out the shape he has traced, then he should be encouraged to do so. In cutting out, he is reinforcing the shape he has already traced out and, in my view, he is experimenting with concepts and symbols—as well as deriving pleasure and satisfaction from achieving something. But never let tracing pictures and shapes take the place of free painting and drawing.

What to expect from children's painting and drawing

Child art follows fairly well-defined stages in development, as Kenneth Jameson and many other experts have shown. No doubt a great deal can be learnt about children's emotional and intellectual levels from their art, but, unless we happen to be psychiatrists with a special interest in discovering something about a disturbed child, it seems to me better not to dabble in the psychoanalysis of child art, but to treat it as a facet of learning through play.

Nevertheless, it is useful to note a few of the stages a child goes through, and for parents who are often trying to push their child on intellectually, it might be especially helpful to realise that no child can by-pass or leapfrog over a particular phase. Every stage has to be experienced and mastered before moving on. It is essential to accept this, since some children will arrive at a certain stage by the age of three, whereas others may be nearly five before they reach it.

The first stage in child art is sometimes known as 'scribbling'. Usually, the scribbles are made by random circular movements of the hand and seem to have no meaning. As we noted in Chapter I, the first explorations of the physical world are frequently made through circular movements of arms and body since these seem to be the natural shape of movement to make. Using his body as a kind of pivot, a child will describe wide, sweeping gestures with his arms, but there is no need to look for any deep and sinister psychological explanation for these movements. They do just come naturally. Hence art at this stage of development is a purely *physical* experience and requires purely physical means to express it. By this I mean the provision of large brushes and large paper—old newspapers will do—for a child to feel, however hesitantly, that his exploratory movements are producing an effect, namely, scribbles and sweeps of colour on the paper.

At the second stage, the scribbling is more controlled. From the exploratory playing with paint, perhaps by accident or perhaps by subconscious design, a child begins to make lines go in the direction he wants them to. No longer haphazard, they begin to *mean* something, at least to him if to no one else.

Thirdly, the controlled scribbles eventually fall into vague but sometimes recognisable shapes and patterns. In this third stage, a child will usually be willing to talk about his drawing or painting. Quite often, he will tell you it is one thing one minute and something else the next. What he is doing is projecting his thinking on to the picture rather as a child *projects* his consciousness on to toys, a process we discussed in Chapter 7. In one sense, then, painting is a form of 'projected play' and, as in junk play and play with natural materials, the child not only projects his thoughts and feelings onto the object, but actually creates it as well. In painting, a child is playing as surely as he is playing with toys or roles or sounds, and by so doing he is learning.

Two basic themes will usually emerge once a degree of physical control over brush, pencil or crayon has been gained. These are the 'man' and the 'house'. Psychiatrists have evolved tests based on the stages apparent in a child's drawing of a man. Perhaps because the circle is a fundamental figure in a child's development both physical and mental, or perhaps because the face is the first part of the body he sees and focuses on, a round figure, possibly with mouth and eyes, represents his early attempts at drawing a man. Legs appear next, coming straight out of the head. The explanation is simple. An under-five most frequently sees only the head or legs of an adult—we often forget that the eye level of a five-year-old's world is only leg-high! As he grows in stature, so does his representation of the human body. After the legs, then the arms, hair, ears and so on.

As the child moves out into the world and he visits different places, so new stimuli affect him and he responds by expressing these new experiences in his fantasy play and in painting. In this way he is 'assimilating and accommodating' his experiences.

Whatever we expect of a child's painting, it can never be more than the child is able to give and that depends on the experiences he is receiving from us as people and from the world around him with all its sights and sounds, textures, tastes and smells. We are at least partially if not wholly responsible for these stimuli, whether as parents, supervisors or teachers and we shall come back to this question of stimuli later.

Facilities for art

In the last three chapters we have said a great deal about what children can make and do with junk, natural materials, paint and paper. But in all these activities, there are obvious problems for the parent who might very well imagine that none of this applies to the home situation.

There is no doubt that facilities for painting and making a mess, as junk play might be described, can be much more easily and conveniently provided in playgroups and schools. Yet it is possible to set up most of these activities in the home, even if they are a little more limited than those in a playgroup. For example, a sheet of polythene can be put down and this will cover the flooring if you want your child to paint. Try to provide a little easel, of which there are many on the market, and paint that easily washes out. Again, this type of paint is easily obtainable. An apron is essential and gives a child confidence because he is no longer worried about dirtying his clothes.

Woodwork in the home is not so easy. Tools need a table, firm but old enough for it not to matter if it gets damaged by saw and hammer. Moreover, a vice is almost essential to hold the wood, because young children do not have the physical strength to hold a piece of wood whilst sawing.

Cutting and pasting are possible if the table and floor are covered with polythene sheeting. And if a room can be set aside for children to play in, make a mess or do whatever they wish, so much the better and then no one need worry at all. Though this may be impossible for most homes, do try to allow some of these activities: they are truly necessary to your child and will give him immense pleasure, encouragement and provide valuable learning situations.

Regarding the provision of facilities in playgroups and schools, there is no need to say any more. All that I have mentioned in connection with the home and throughout the last three chapters applies in more organised situations, only more so.

And one last word of advice and warning about all children's work. What a child has made is precious, a treasure, and it belongs to him. So do remember that it is a private world that he is making public in telling you about what he has done. Respect that world and respect his creation. In turn, he will come to respect you and your possessions, and in a wider context, other peoples' rights and possessions in the world. This is part of the whole process of learning to live.

We can end this chapter with the words of Kenneth Jameson. 'Is the art of the young child art or non-art? It is neither. It is pictorial language . . . He wants to tell everybody about his own social experiences in the world. At his age he has no thought of making a work of art. He wants to communicate and he uses his brush and his paint, his pencil and paper and his "visual symbol" language to do it.'

11 Music play

Music, like painting, writing and making things of any kind, is a means of expressing feelings and ideas and communicating those feelings and ideas to other people. Music can be a private or a public experience. It can be enjoyed by an individual or shared with others.

According to my definition of play as an exploratory and communicative experience, music is play, and like all forms of play, it can take us out of ourselves, providing an escape into a world of sound and rhythms; or it can help us to discover and explore all kinds of sounds ranging from those made by the human voice to those hammered out with a spoon on a plate. And even if spoon banging is not our idea of music we must try to understand some of the modern trends in the concept of music, particularly the one set by the American, John Cage, who claims to hear music in every possible sound.

We should at least appreciate that an under-five's idea of music may not be ours. For one thing, his hearing is not sufficiently sensitive nor his voice sufficiently developed to cope with the wide range of intricate sounds involved in making, playing and listening to music. We have, then, to start from the point of view that all children need music as a personal experience of 'Escape, Recovery and Consolation'. We must be convinced that music really does have these effects, if we are to get anywhere at all with music play for under-fives.

The meaning of music for under-fives

But what kind of music for under-fives? Or rather, what does music mean to the under-five? A simple answer to this question is very much in line with John Cage's claims—everything! Because everything has a fascination for a young child, he needs to bang and scrape, to clap his hands and stamp his feet, to squeak and squeal as well as talk and sing, to blow bubbles with or without a pipe and to experiment with that delightful sound made by blowing through a straw instead of sucking! These are sounds of his new world and he must have a chance to find out about them, whether he makes them himself or whether they are made by other people and other things.

In fact, everything that surrounds him can produce a sound of some sort. When considering the place of music in the life of an under-five, we may have to change quite radically our opinions as to what music is. So we might begin by trying to relate some of the points made earlier about children's development to some of their common attitudes towards music.

In the first place, rhythm rather than melody appeals to an under-five. Musical tones are not widely differentiated in the early years as anyone who has listened to a group of under-fives singing will no doubt have realised.

Rhythm, however, is fundamental to every child's life. You may remember that in Chapter 1 I pointed out that the heartbeat is the earliest rhythm a child experiences: first his mother's, then his own. And the rhythm of the heartbeat is one which young children quickly follow. It is, of course, the rhythm of the march, and marching rhythm, whether as a piece of recorded music or beaten out on drum for children to listen to, or actually played by them, is one that they always take delight in. This is their kind of music and we should provide opportunities for them to experience it for themselves, even if the noise does become aggravating at times. Most of us are only conscious of our heart beating or the rhythm of our breathing when something abnormal occurs. But these are fundamental rhythms and are

Making one's own rhythm.

expressed either in formal, composed musical rhythms, or the informal, spontaneous activities of foot stamping, hand clapping, banging of drum, tin can, table or whatever.

The second point about music and under-fives is that the rhythm not only echoes their heartbeat, but is also predictable. By this I mean that pleasure and satisfaction are derived from the realisation that one beat follows another at regular and definite intervals. And whether a child actually makes the rhythm himself or whether it is made for him and he joins in by tapping, stamping or clapping, there is satisfaction in discovering not only that he is the cause, that he can make an event happen, but that he can also make it happen in a definite and predictable way. Thus, for an under-five the rhythmic element in music is meeting his basic need to express himself in a definite and consequently satisfying way.

Moreover, rhythm, as we noticed in Chapter I, is felt by the child in the womb and later, when mother rocks him in her arms, cradle, cot or pram, the motion is recreated for him. This rhythm continues throughout life. Folk plays and other ritual dance drama throughout the world express the adult's hunger for predictable and definite patterns in living. Children, too, are essentially ritualists, gaining self-confidence in routines in which they dislike being disturbed. No child likes the repetitive pattern of a story or rhythmic movement destroyed any more than he likes his patterns of life upset by moving house or school or changing meal times. Because children are such ritualists, their singing and dancing games often preserve the seasonal events of the natural world in ritual form, and this leads us to note a few points about the relationship of singing and dancing to music.

Singing

Singing involves melody as well as rhythm and for young children, the simple nursery rhyme with or without piano accompaniment provides an opportunity to explore tones and tunes in a very elementary way, but a way which is well within their capabilities. A piano is useful but not essential. Do remember that the human voice is just as much an instrument as an electronic organ.

One sad feature of modern life with its incessant background of music in home, at work, supermarkets and restaurants is that so many parents have lost the art of singing to their children.

The lullaby is based on sound psychology. Mother's familiar voice, the warmth of her arms and body, the gentle rocking motion suggested by the rhythm of the song all contributed to her baby's sense of well-being. And later, when there were 'songs at mother's knee' where children learnt a great deal about the joys and griefs of life, singing was often a preparation for life. This is another example of one of the functions of play in general, namely to re-create and restore emotional balance and a sense of security.

Songs that record or comment on human experience may be stored in the memory and are potential means for children to express themselves either as individuals or with others. So, if you have any sort of voice, do try singing to your children. Apart from anything else, what you sing is part of their heritage.

Dancing

Young children dance rather than walk, not perhaps in the formal

Singing together.

124

style adults associate with dancing, but in a way that expresses joy in their continually increasing physical powers. And nearly always the expression of these powers is in rhythmic form. Hence, marching—a dance of sorts, surely—or rhythms that are clear and strong will encourage a more formal expression of the need to use the body. Formal rhythm helps children control their body movements which at first will be uncoordinated and clumsy.

Of course, in dancing or in moving generally, children are also using the sensori–motor process of learning which, as we have seen before, is vital to the young child. In dance, children are learning through movement, learning to control their arms, legs and bodies, and if when listening to music they begin to dance, or at least to move in some sort of co-ordinated rhythmic manner, then they should be encouraged to do so. As a child grows, so the control of his body movements increases and he becomes capable of experiencing more complicated rhythms and expressing them in more formal and controlled dance or movement forms. For the under-fives, then, a strong, easily recognised rhythm to which they can march, jump or skip is the kind we should try to provide.

Music and language

Earlier I remarked that the human voice is a musical instrument; now we can take this remark a step further, by saying that the voice plays the tunes of a language. Every language is a form of music consisting of rhythm, tone and stress. The English language is essentially a stressed language with a marked rhythm of its own. By 'stressed' I mean that we place an emphasis on certain syllables in words or on particular words in a sentence.

When we talk we can even change the meaning of what we say by changing the stress. 'You're a fine boy, you are!' can be interpreted in at least two ways, depending on where the stress is laid. If, for example, we stress the 'You're' and the 'you', there is a strong sense of irony and, in fact, we probably imply the exact opposite of what the printed words indicate. On the other hand, if we stress 'fine', we mean what we say. In print or writing we have to add a word like 'ironically' or 'sarcastically' to show precisely what is meant by the written sentence. In speech we can show this by tone and stress.

The whole business of speech and language was discussed in Chapter 4, but we can now add the dimension of music to the development of children's speech, because music is very closely related to the rhythmic element in speech and exploring musical rhythms can be a help in learning the rhythms of speech, the give and take, the ebb and flow of conversation, so much of which depends upon interpreting the rhythmic stress signals. One way of teaching children their own names and the names of other children, teachers and playgroup supervisors and helpers, is to tap out the rhythm of the name. Language, then, is the music played by the instrument of the human voice and we have to learn its tunes, tones and stresses if we want to become fluent in speech. The rhythms of music play can help a great deal in this respect.

Music and action

Finger play, in which the content of the song or rhyme is interpreted with fingers, hands and arms, is also an excellent means of developing the co-ordination of mind and body, and, of course, the sensori-motor learning process again underlies the activity. Examples of these finger play rhymes are many and varied. There are such well known favourites as 'Two little dickey birds sat on a wall', 'Incey mincey spider', 'Tommy Thumb' and so on. And these rhymes can also be a useful introduction to simple counting.

Using finger play to interpret both content and rhythmic form, like counting and the tapping out of names and funny-sounding words—'alligator' is a delight—and clapping and stamping, are all aspects of music play for the under-fives.

Listening to music

One more general point about music concerns listening to pieces of music for their own sake. A child's attitudes to life are usually the reflection of what he hears in his own home, and music is no exception. The four-year-old whom I heard singing, with surprising musical ability, 'Bring me sunshine' had obviously been up late and watched *The Morecambe and Wise Show*, and the music had stuck in his mind. And it may very well be that to surround a child with musical experiences is equally as important as to surround him with books. The results may not be so obvious but they are just as helpful.

A piece of music that tells a story and stimulates mental

pictures may not satisfy the musical connoisseur, but it goes down well with an under-five. Saints-Saens's *Carnival of the Animals*, in which the musical instruments echo the animals' voices or Prokofiev's *Peter and the Wolf*, which has recognisable themes or motifs to identify characters in the story, are both examples of the narrative picture-type of music young children can appreciate. And because the emphasis is on sound and melody rather than rhythm, these are excellent pieces for children to listen to.

In a playgroup, however, it might be possible to interpret some aspects of the music in action which verges on drama, though I do not personally believe that drama has much relevance for children under five for reasons I gave in Chapter 6. All young children's play is a form of drama or vice versa. Nevertheless, some music can stimulate simple movement such as tip-toeing through the forest or growing into trees from little seeds.

And do remember that silence is not only golden but as much a part of music as sound. Every sound we make when speaking is separated by a fraction of silence. If it were not so, our speech would be meaningless. And silence sharpens our awareness of sounds. Composers know all about the value of the silent bar as a means of creating suspense and surprise, and the pauses made by public speakers are usually the prelude to the most significant points they want to make. Listen to great actors: the rhythms of their speech, especially their pauses and silences, are equally as important as the sound of the words.

In these noisy days, we all need silence and we need to listen for it! This, I think, is the reason why a little book like Ruth Ainsworth and Ronald Ridout's *What can you hear?* is so useful. Though designed to be read *by* children, it can become the inspiration for a game depending on the ritual repetition of 'Don't move a hand, don't move a foot, shut your eyes and sit very still. What can you hear?' The book indicates a number of things, clocks ticking, aeroplanes, bees buzzing and so on. But children will hear all sorts of things and by listening they can be made aware not only of the silence and the stillness, but also of the innumerable sounds that continually surround them. Some of these sounds are so soft that we often miss hearing them altogether. This is the music of the world, the child's world, and his ears need to be sensitive to pick up the tiny sounds of life. The game also 'teaches' children to sit still and listen. Sound and silence, rhythm and movement, speech and song—these are all aspects of music, and are necessary for the emotional, intellectual and physical developments of children. How to provide children with the necessary musical experiences is best looked at from two points of view: the first dealing with the individual child in the home and the second dealing with the child in the playgroup or school.

Music in the home

Most of what needs to be said about music in the home also applies to music in a group, though there are obviously some activities that can be done in a group which cannot take place at home. For example, marching on one's own is not nearly as much fun as in a group and some of the movement work suggested above is not really effective for an individual child at home.

In the home, music play can take two main forms: music to move to and music to listen to. And in certain situations, we can combine the two so as to listen and move at the same time.

Instruments can be made from practically anything and we might have mentioned them when we were discussing junk play, because instruments used in rhythmic accompaniment can easily be made out of junk. Plastic bottles filled with pebbles, rice, sand, dried peas or anything that will rattle are excellent, and are really versions of the South American maraccas, which make a delightfully satisfying noise.

Chime bars and xylophones can be used not only for rhythms but also for the introduction of tones and tunes. Drums and tambourines, either bought or made from tins with lids taped on and a string threaded through for carrying, are, of course, favourites with children though, understandably, not always with parents! Nevertheless, within the limits of toleration, children ought to have a chance to play drums, tambourines and shakers at home, especially if it can be included as part of their natural play as well as in a more formal musical setting when they try to accompany a piece of music on the radio or record player.

Other instruments that children love to play are triangles, cymbals and bells. Since bells are rhythmic they are pleasant to listen to as well as to play.

But in the home other aspects of music might be even more important. Thus singing is something all children should experience. If the singing is accompanied by finger play, we shall be combining two activities in one: the pleasure of rhythm and tune and the sensori-motor aspect of learning. *This Little Puffin,* a book of nursery rhymes and finger play, is a most useful collection of traditional pieces and some which might not be so well known. No home, playgroup or school should be without a copy!

Music for listening to is very important. If children hear nothing but radio programmes with the incessant talk of disc jockeys, their musical experience will be severely limited. Occasionally, play them music of the kind described earlier: pieces which tell a story. You will be surprised at what children *do* like, especially if they try to identify the instruments making particular sounds: a trumpet, a drum, a violin and so on. There are several books about music and musical instruments designed for under-fives, one of the best being in the Macdonald *Starters* series, a series, incidentally, which we shall be looking at in the next chapter dealing with books.

Music in the playgroup

Everything that has been said about music in the home also applies here, but more so! There are obviously many different activities you can enjoy in a group that you cannot do on your own.

For example, singing in a group can be accompanied by singing games. Doing things together is part of co-operative play and within the structure of the game there is room for personal manoeuvre and individual expression. These are the reasons why there are so many games of the singing, dancing kind usually known as 'ring games', in which a circle is the basic figure. Many of these singing games preserve very ancient folklore, but this is purely incidental and much of the lore has been forgotten if not lost completely. Children however, still find great satisfaction in dancing and singing together in a ring game.

The Little Puffin has many suggestions for these games and Peter and Iona Opie's classic book on children's games, *The Lore and Language of Schoolchildren*, is a mine of information and reminds many of us of the games we once played and have since forgotten. Indeed, adults can get as much fun out of joining in a game like 'The Farmer's in His Den' as any of the children. And I would add here that the adult's function in most of these activities is to be the focus of order, a kind of 'referee' who is there to see that the rules are properly kept, but to take part in the game at the same time. Children love to see an adult identifying with their fun, though it must be done without condescension.

One form of music which has resulted in recent years from the advance of technology is that made by what are called 'electronic synthesisers'. There are many recordings of this type of music and children really do enjoy listening and moving to the unfamiliar sounds. Some of these are in groups of rising and falling notes described as 'growth shapes' and some have rhythmic bases to which melodic 'tunes' are added bit by bit. Electronic music is very useful for introducing movement work. The first type of sound lends itself to stretching and growing, or shrinking and curling up. Used for a very elementary form of dance/drama, this kind of sound is excellent. The rhythmic type needs very little comment. Some sequences suggest fiery dragons spitting and clawing, and thus give children the chance to work off some of their aggressive energies. Electronic sounds should be available in every playgroup, and a child will also enjoy listening to the 'funny sounds' on his own although they are not so effective for use in the home.

When to play music for children to listen to as a group can present a bit of a problem. There will always be some children who say they do not want to listen. In these cases, we have to help them to acquire the listening habit. The game we referred to earlier based on the words: 'Don't move a hand, don't move a foot . . .' can work astonishingly well in producing silence. Then the music can be played.

Always tell children a little about the music they are going to hear. Give them something specific to listen for; it might be a particular little tune, a special rhythm or an instrument that the children can identify. But never play too long a piece. The same advice applies to music as to stories: keep it short! Better for children to want more than to become quickly bored through having to listen for too long. Five to ten minutes will be quite sufficient for them.

Finally, it is a very good idea to have a music corner where instruments are left out for children to experiment with. Most first schools already have such corners and though the exploration may sound chaotic and confusing for a while, the results of random exploration are often surprising. If we need to measure musical results, we can do so by the degree of absorption and interest the children display in making and listening to music.

In music play, we are laying foundations for musical experiences which, like all play forms, are part of the human heritage and an integral part of every society in the world. Wherever there are human beings, there are rhythm and melody, for rhythm and melody are fundamental to life itself.

12 Books

Books are the tools and toys of the mind. In story play, a book is, in effect, a toy with which children imaginatively explore the world of fantasy—and fantasy play, as we have seen, is vital both to learning about life in general and to our emotional well-being in particular. Some books, however, may be more like tools which we use to probe for information and ideas, testing what we have discovered for ourselves against the discoveries of experts. And until technology finds a way of making cheap, personal computers for storing facts, books will remain a major source of information. I remember an eminent professor of education once remarking that 'education is not knowing the facts but knowing where to find them', and I believe this to be absolutely true. Many of us just do not know how to go about searching for an answer to a purely factual problem. Unfamiliar with libraries, or unaccustomed to fishing for information, we wallow helplessly in an ocean of books. Where do we begin to sort it all out? Mainly, I think, we need to develop the habit of consulting books early in life, so that a book becomes as familiar to us as a toothbrush. And this is where the home, playgroup and first school have such important parts to play.

The reason for stressing the need to start early with books is that, especially for the under-fives, toys are tools and vice-versa. You may remember we discussed the identity that young children make of work and play, so that they do not distinguish between 'playing at work' or 'working at play'. Hence, a tool intended for *work* is just as likely to be used as a toy for the *imagination* to play with. What is a hammer one minute may be a gun the next! Work and play, tool and toy, this is the delightful confusion which makes books so natural and so much fun for children to use— with one important proviso. If there are no books in the home, then the chances are that children will not find it easy to transfer what they do in playgroup or school to their home. We shall be talking about this dual attitude to social customs in the following chapter.

The habit of reading, of consulting books and of finding in them the release from the emotional tensions of life can begin as soon as a child is capable of holding a book in his hands. In this chapter, we shall be dealing with the kind of books that fulfil specific purposes, the shape and feel of books and a few hints on methods of storytelling. Also included is a short, representative list of books that seem to meet particular needs. But I must add that a book which goes down well with one child or one group of children on one day might not be successful with other children on other days. I am not at all sure why this happens, but from experience I know that it is so. Maybe it has something to do with the children's different backgrounds of experience, differences in temperament and so on, but the fact remains that *some* books are always favourites; others vary in their appeal.

Books and their functions

We have already mentioned two very broad functions of books, namely, to meet our needs for fantasy on the one hand, and for information on the other. We can now subdivide these functions into more specific ones. What I must emphasise in all that follows is the quality of enjoyment that should accompany the experience of story books or information books. We must try to avoid the somewhat old-fashioned approach to books, which was inspired by the belief that books should somehow 'do children good'. We have, I hope, left the obviously 'moral tale' far behind, and are now much more likely to provide a book in which the moral, if there is one, is presented in the form of a parable. So enjoyment is a common factor I take for granted in considering the particular appeal of every kind of book we shall be discussing.

A second point, which I also take for granted, is that from time to time there should be a sharing of this enjoyment. Whether it is talking about the information and ideas in the book, or about the characters in the stories or any other topics that arise from looking at a book together, part of the enjoyment in any experience is sharing it with someone else. And children will delight in telling you what they have found or what they can see in the pictures, even if they cannot read the text. But the actual methods of using books, when children should read books on their own and when they should have books read to them, we shall deal with later. Bearing these two major points in mind, we can now move on to look at particular functions of books.

You will remember that when we discussed the function of stories in an earlier chapter, I suggested that stories fell very roughly into three categories, namely, myth, parable or fable and stories of everyday life. I admit, however, that many stories fall into all three or none at all but, purely for convenience, I think the categories are useful. Leaving aside for the moment the question of books for information, we shall turn firstly to a few examples of books that seem to me to illustrate the points I made earlier about myth, parable and stories of everyday life.

Myths and fairy tales

In her excellent book on *Literature and the Young Child*, Joan Cass remarks on the human hunger for making sense of the universe, a theme we dealt with in the chapter on story play. 'A very important human need is security, to feel safely protected and provided for, for the world must have seemed a cruel and hostile place to human beings, and still does, full of things they could neither understand nor explain . . . It is not surprising, therefore, to have countless stories and myths where the elements take on human form and behave in a human way, when a god rises from the sea or drives the chariots of the sun across the sky.' Furthermore, as Joan Cass points out, animals may be symbolic figures standing for parents or other frightening characters in real or imagined life.

A myth, then, as we saw earlier, is a story that attempts to make sense of the universe. For under-fives, the wider implications of the meaning of existence and the origins of mankind are not particularly relevant, but two books are worth noting because they do deal with some common experiences of the young child.

The first example is *Anansi the Spider*, one of the traditional tales from Ghana in West Africa that has also become well established in the West Indies. Anansi is a mythical spider whose function is clearly to explain the origins of earth and sky, human beings and so on. In the story as retold by Gerald McDermott, the myth concerns the beginnings of man on earth and includes some fairly obvious hints that the world exists to be *shared*. Without going into details, the theme of the story revolves around the question of which son shall inherit his father's land. The conclusion reached is that it should not be inherited by any particular one of them, but that it is for everyone.

The second example is a variation of Jack and the Beanstalk called *Jim and the Beanstalk* by Raymond Briggs. Here is a mythological story based on the necessity for young and therefore physically *small* children to come to terms with grown-ups or the *large* people. Giants, a favourite theme of the mythical and legendary story, are probably projections of a child's fear of the grown-up whose world he feels is too big for him. In brief, Jim climbs a beanstalk, meets the giant, eats his breakfast with him, and discovers that the giant needs a new pair of glasses and a wig for his bald head. Jim measures him up for these items and gets them for him from his own world at the bottom of the beanstalk. As soon as the giant puts on the wig and glasses, he feels younger and hungry. He looks at Jim and considers the possibility of eating 'fried boy'. Jim waits for no more, but slides down the beanstalk. He then cuts it down with an axe, because he can hear 'the thunder of the Giant's footsteps', which are perhaps an echo of 'father's footsteps'! Just as the beanstalk falls, a huge piece of paper comes down wrapped around a gold coin. The paper thanks Jim for his help, and his mother says that he can keep a coin for himself. Maybe, by owning a coin, he has grown up a little, but he has certainly made contact with and come to some understanding of the giant, grown-up world.

A third example, which seems to me an excellent idea, but which ends in a disastrous misunderstanding of the function of myth and fantasy, is Margaret Mahy's *A Lion in the Meadow*. Beautifully illustrated, the story may be summarised by the publisher's blurb: 'A lion in the meadow? Yes, a lion in the meadow. And although the lion was fierce and whiskery he became the little boy's friend. Together they felt safe from the dragon. A dragon? In the meadow, too? Yes . . .' The story concerns the way the boy's mother invents a dragon to deal with the child's invented lion. And both become 'real' to the boy who makes friends with the lion. But 'the mother never ever made up a story again'. What a dreadful shame! The story delightfully deals with the common experience of young children who do have very real fears of monsters and fierce, biting animals, and whose fears can be dealt with in story form. Not to make up stories is to deny the ancient function of myth and maybe destroy the possibility of overcoming fear. Watch out for any approach to fantasy which does not take it seriously—and avoid it!

In the chapter on story play, we also considered the function of folk and fairy tales and I pointed out then that, structurally, they frequently depend upon three incidents, three characters, three tasks and so on. I also suggested that the emphasis on the number three was possibly a reflection of the basic family unit, mother, father and child. But there is also another element in tales of this kind and that is 'the journey'. All young children seem to delight in the repetitive quality of words and incidents and love to hear about the journey which, for all we know, may symbolise their own journey into the world where there are indeed tasks to perform and fears to overcome. But we need not bother too much over the psychology of the fairy tale here, except to emphasise the perennial fascination of these tales. All children should hear about 'The Three Bears', 'Three Billy Goats Gruff' and 'The Three Little Pigs'. In fact, despite the many excellent modern fairy tales being written, it is my experience that children still want to go back to 'The Three Bears'! There is, of course, a sense of security in the familiar and the predictable, so we must never overlook or neglect the traditional fairy tale because we, the storytellers, have become bored with it. What bores us to death may give life to a child! And it is his world we must be concerned about, not ours.

'Parabolic' stories or fables with a moral

There are literally hundreds of books of parabolic stories and fables. In this type, as you will remember, one purpose is to help children come to terms with actual problems and events in their lives. All I can do here is refer to a few of these typical problems and give the titles of some story books which deal with them.

Parabolic stories often have an animal setting. For example *Harry the Dirty Dog* by Gene Zion is a parable of 'cleanliness'. A white dog with black spots is unrecognised because he gets dirty and turns black with white spots. So he has to be washed, the implication being that washing makes everyone at home happy. *A House for Jones*, by Helen Cresswell, concerns a rabbit called Jones who tries to find a new house because he does not like living in a burrow. Various animals, birds and insects offer him their homes, but since he cannot get into a mousehole, fly into a tree or swim in the pond, these homes are no use to him. Eventually he settles for a haystack which he shares with all the creatures he has met in the story. Perhaps this is a story that could ease a child into the new experience of moving into a high-rise flat.

The dangers of wandering far from home are implied in Dick Bruna's *Pussy Nell*. Pussy Nell finds home is best after her visit to the Red Indians, as does Rosie in *Rosie's Walk* by Pat Hutchins. Rosie is a chicken who wanders off followed by a fox. She manages to keep out of trouble and arrive home safely after her adventures. This particular book has simple words, but children can understand the meaning of the story by looking at the pictures on their own. The security of different kinds of home is the thinly disguised 'message' of *The Animals' Lullaby* by Trude Alberti. Security for a child is assured at the end of the story with the words: 'Who is singing a lullaby to the baby asleep in the cradle?' His mother and father are singing softly 'Sleep, my little one, sleep'. And incidentally, this little book could very well support the singing of actual lullabies, the importance of which we noted in the previous chapter.

Children dealing with common problems and everyday events are used in Leila Berg's *Nipper* series. We discussed the language of these stories in an earlier chapter, but the content of these books is excellent, and their form ideal. In *Hospital Day*, for example, Nan pays a visit to the hospital for treatment, and she ends up by saying 'Lovely it was, talking away with all my mates on hospital day'. So a child may be reconciled to the idea of a visit to hospital himself.

Peter's Chair by Ezra Jack Keats deals with the common and very important problem of the new baby. Peter is upset because his mother is preparing a cradle which was once his, his father is painting a chair that also belonged to him and so on. He feels displaced and talks to his dog about running away. And how many children have either said this or actually done it! But Peter realises that his old cradle and chair are far too small for him, so he decides to help instead of hinder. This is an excellent parabolic story using a real-life rather than a symbolic setting.

'Schoolphobia' is very common amongst children, especially the rising-fives who are about to leave the security of their home or playgroup and move on to a first school. Apart from visits to the school to prepare the way, stories can help to some extent. Thus, a book like *Lucy and Tom Go to School* by Shirley Hughes is well worth reading to children. Lucy goes to school but there is fighting and rough behaviour at playtime which upsets her. The matter is eventually sorted out, but in the meantime, Tom goes to his playgroup. The book therefore deals with the new and probably frightening experience of going to a big school and the experience of a younger brother or sister whose compensation for the loss of his playmate is to go to *his* version of school. The *Topsy and Tim* Series by Jean and Gareth Adamson are also excellent, dealing with problems like 'schoolphobia' and the new baby.

These examples do not by any means exhaust either the books dealing with the problems mentioned or, indeed, all the problems a child is likely to have. However, this short account should give some idea of the way parabolic stories and fables can help children in their process of learning to live.

Stories of everyday life

As we discussed earlier in the chapter on story play, the function of true-to-life stories is to reinforce what children are learning about their world. All children take great delight in listening to a story that could very well be about them, but such stories also help to put into perspective what the child has experienced so that he can build on them new structures of thought, or schemas.

For example, Leila Berg's *Little Pete* stories, which are ideal for reading to children, recount the adventures of a little boy who is gradually penetrating the secrets of the world around him. *Let's Go Shopping*, a story without words prepared by the Pre-

School Playgroup Association, is a useful little book for generating conversation. The pictures are self-explanatory and can be followed by a child looking at them without adult guidance.

Bedtime is often a problem and must be prepared for. As I have stressed in earlier chapters, it is always necessary to let children's play run down slowly before it finally comes to an end. Bedtime usually includes the bathing or washing period and not all children take pleasure in getting wet! So a book like *Thomas has a bath* by Gunilla Wolde, which in some ways reinforces the parabolic story of washing in *Harry the Dirty Dog* already mentioned, is helpful because a child can identify with this bathing situation.

Sleep itself can also be a problem sometimes. A book that not only tells a tale but also introduces an element of parable is *Frances the Face-Maker*, by William Cole and Toni Ungerer. This book deals with the reluctant sleeper and treats going to bed as fun.

It can be used as a bedtime story and the picture of Frances asleep in her bed is followed by the final page showing a picture of an open window and the moon with the words 'You do it!' Maybe some children will do it sometimes! But the book itself is quite delightful. Again this question of going to sleep can be dealt with by the parabolic story, *The Animal's Lullaby*, noted earlier.

Remember that it is always possible to invent a simple narrative about everyday life. No complicated plot is necessary; merely relate the incidents that you know from experience could happen and perhaps *have* happened to a child during the course of a morning. A description of routine events is all that is really needed, such as getting up, eating breakfast, going for a walk with mother, seeing various people on the way and so on. The *Topsy and Tim* series is based on this very principle.

Information books

There is very little to say about this section because the function of the information book is obvious. Books should be chosen for the simple way the information is presented; big, bold pictures with a minimum of text is the rule for under-fives' information books. Books of this type can be a talking point with children; or mothers and playgroup leaders can use them by asking a child to go and get a piece of information from a book on the shelf or in the book corner. This will be teaching him in a very elementary way how to search out facts.

There are now so many well designed series of information books that it is quite impossible to mention all of them. Here, then, are just a few. Particularly good are the Macdonald *Starters* of which there is a very wide range available including such titles as *Cars, Farms, Clothes, Night* (a very useful one since children are fascinated by and frightened of the dark), *Toys, Snow, Sleep, Music* and *Homes*. Methuen's *Look Around* series written by Alain Gree has titles like *Look what smokes* and *Look what goes round*. Macmillan's collection of *See how it grows* books with titles like *The butterfly* and *The seed* have beautiful, self-explanatory illustrations and children do not have to read even the very simple text beneath each picture in order to understand the meaning.

A series not strictly fitting into this section is *A book for me to read,* by Ruth Ainsworth and Ronald Ridout. Each book has good pictures and varying degrees of difficulty in the text. A pre-reading child can get enjoyment out of looking at and talking about the pictures, whilst in a first school, children just beginning to read can cope with the simple text very easily. Especially useful is *What can you hear?* noted in the previous chapter on music, *What are they?* which deals with different occupations, *Susan's House,* which has pictures based on a child's attempts at drawing a house, and *Colours.*

Poetry books

Before turning to the more practical aspects of books, we must say something about poetry for under-fives. As non-readers, however, under-fives cannot do very much about poetry on their own, so that poetry books, though available on the shelves, will almost certainly have to be read to children by parents or supervisors. Personally, I believe poetry works better with under-fives if it is read to them in a group rather than to individuals. There is some sort of 'collective' enjoyment, a sharing of the fun and the rhythms that is not so easy to generate on one's own.

Nevertheless, all young children should have some experience of poetry. Most probably this will be mainly of the finger play and action rhyme types. Nursery rhymes must certainly have a place, too. In fact, for the under-fives, poetry is closely linked with music, a point we discussed in the previous chapter. Children will also enjoy Edward Lear's *Quangle Wangle* and other nonsense verse simply because the sound of the words appeals to them, and this is another reason for closely linking poetry for the under-fives with music.

For finger play and action rhymes, *This Little Puffin* is an excellent book and includes the music if you decide to sing the rhymes instead of merely saying them. There are many collections of nursery rhymes, but perhaps *The Oxford Nursery Rhyme Book* edited by Iona and Peter Opie is one of the best. Spike Milligan's *Silly Verse for Kids* might also be worth a try, though it is perhaps more suitable for slightly older children.

Finally, under-fives ought to have contact at some stage with what I would call more 'literary' poems. Occasionally, during a moment of quiet, slip in a simple, short poem as a comment on the weather or some other topical subject. A delightful little collection of poems and action rhymes is *Come Follow Me: Poems for the Very Young*, or Leila Berg's *Four Feet and Two*. There are beautifully illustrated editions of Edward Lear's *Quangle Wangle* and *The Owl and the Pussycat*, both of which children can look at after the poems have been read to them.

Poetry is as much a part of our culture as stories, so do give children the chance to enjoy it. Under-fives usually do!

The function of books in relation to reading

So far we have been mainly concerned with the content of books and their imaginative and informative aspects. Only incidentally have we mentioned such questions as to how much a child can understand of a book without his being able to read it. Some books, of course, are intended for children in the pre-reading stage, the authors basing their approach on the fact that written language is not the only means of communication. Pictures and symbols, as we saw in the chapter on language and story play, communicate meaning and always have done. So for very young children, some books are designed to present their meaning through pictures, shapes and symbols, whilst others deliberately set out to introduce children to the skill of reading. Such techniques as recognising different shapes lead on to the eventual recognition of the different shapes of letters. But books should not be used merely as technical devices for the teaching of reading.

This is rather like repeating some of the meaningless sentences and words which used to appear in the old reading books of the nineteenth century. If a book is uninteresting, no one can be expected to want to read it.

Going a very long way towards meeting this need for interest is a series of colourful little books which does seem to represent something of a breakthrough into the pre-reading world of the under-fives. This is Terry Hall's *Laugh and Learn* series which has titles like *Silly me, Crash! Bang!* and *Oh! Gosh!* Each of the stories tells about the adventures of Bushy the squirrel. The text in each book becomes progressively more difficult, but for the child who cannot read at all, the vivid and sharply drawn pictures tell their own stories. Bushy gets into some fearful scrapes and the slapstick, farcical fun is just what young children need to stimulate interest and the wish to go on learning to read. Having tried this series out on a group of under-fives I know that, after a while, many of the children, without any formal teaching of letters, could begin to identify words simply by associating a word with its pictures.

Two other books are worth mentioning here as typical, firstly of those books deliberately intended for the pre-reader, and secondly of those that might introduce children to the shape of words as they associate a word with a picture.

Changes, Changes by Pat Hutchins has no words at all. The theme is based on children's delight in playing with coloured building bricks. So each picture shows a different construction including engines and houses, but each example uses the same blocks. Children can therefore learn to recognise shapes in different positions, and this is necessary for pre-reading skills. On the other hand, the book can be a talking point without children having to bother about the techniques of reading at all.

The second example is a book I have found most successful with under-fives. This is *The Toolbox* by Anne and Harlow Rockwell. In a sense this is a book of the information type, merely describing the contents of a toolbox. There are bold pictures of a hammer, a saw, sandpaper and a work bench with a little boy helping his father. The text is absolutely basic but meaningful. Yet it is not necessary to read to comprehend what the book is about. It is an excellent pre-reading book in which a few simple words are introduced.

Never force a child to try to read the text. And do not be

worried by the fact that the neighbour's child can apparently read when yours cannot! As I have mentioned before children do not develop 'reading readiness' at precisely the same age and they also learn in different ways. Some can visualise better than they can hear and may take longer to identify shapes than another child. Nevertheless, you may be very surprised to discover just how many words a child is able to recognise, and if he is doing no more than beginning to see the difference in the shape of letters, this will be a great step forward.

The appearance of books

There are many factors involved in considering the appearance or presentation of books: such questions as what the print looks like and how well it relates to the pictures. As a matter of interest, the right-hand page, as advertisers know very well, is the more dominant one which we tend to look at first. So, depending on whether you think the picture or the print is more important, this might be some sort of criterion for deciding on the appeal of a particular book.

Then there are such factors as cost, the shape and even the feel of the paper. With regard to cost, the larger illustrated books like the beautifully produced examples by Brian Wildsmith are typical of the higher priced category. There is no doubt that children do like to handle large, attractive books, and for the telling of a story to a group of children, this type of book with its big, clear illustrations is almost essential. Personally, I prefer books like this to have the text quite distinct from the picture, though, unfortunately in my opinion, considerations of artistic design and lay-out often cause a publisher to overprint picture with print. I cannot always read the text easily myself let alone any child just starting out on the road to reading.

Perhaps the answer to the problem of expense with large books is for children to own one or two themselves, but for play-groups to keep a wide selection for group storytelling and talking points. And if parents or playgroups cannot afford many of these books, the local library will lend them. But in these days many paperback versions are also available and for most people, these meet the demand for cheap books. Many of these are well designed, being strong enough to withstand the wear and tear an under-five or a playgroup is likely to give them. The *Picture*

Puffins, for example, are attractive and large enough for small children to handle. But do not forget that children also like to hold small books, because these are like their miniature fantasy world—manageable! Sometimes, however, the text and pictures in small books are not big enough for children to see. Avoid the obviously badly produced cheap book. Better to have *one* worthwhile, well designed book than two or three poor ones. Children need to recognise the value of something well done and they can learn to recognise this from what you provide for them.

Finally, a word about colour. Young children see bold colours and sharply defined patterns. What may seem to be an ingenious illustration to adults will be so much confusion to an under-five. The strength of Dick Bruna's *Miffy* series and others like it is that the design is bold, clear, uncomplicated and colourful. As Joan Cass so rightly points out: 'Children under six or seven tend to see "wholes", so figures in pictures need to be strong and clear in outline, otherwise they may appear just as a lot of unrelated detail.'

In deciding on what books to buy, apart from their content, try to keep in mind some of the points we have mentioned. And you could perhaps also bear in mind how you expect the book to be used.

The use of books

Obviously, books can be used by the child on his own and we should always provide some form of easy access to a collection of of books, either his own on a bookshelf or those belonging to a playgroup in the book corner. On the other hand, books can be used by parents, playgroup leaders or teachers for storytelling or for a talking point and the beginning of conversation, not forgetting, of course, that all books are useful for pure pleasure!

Information books can be consulted by an individual child and he can come and tell you about what he has found out. Try not to help him too much, but let him search out the material for himself. But if he gets into difficulties and becomes frustrated be on hand to give reassurance and advice. There is not much more to say about the use of this type of book, except to stress the need to talk over what he sees in the pictures and try to answer the questions he asks. Dealing with story books, however, will take a little longer.

Reading is fun.

We tell stories either to an individual child or to a group of children. In the former case, the bedtime story told by mother or father conveys the reassuring feeling that all is well before a child goes to sleep. Of course, bedtime is not the only time for telling stories, but it is certainly a moment to be treasured, as all those of us who have experienced bedtime stories know very well.

Sometimes mother might invent a story especially if it is the 'parabolic' type and she wants to deal with a particular problem facing her child; more usually, though, she will read from a book. And as we have been saying, books that spark off the child's interest are the best kind and you may not get beyond the first page because there is so much to talk about. Nevertheless, reading a straight-forward story without interruption, especially familiar fairy tales, is the method I would always advocate.

There are two ways of dealing with group storytelling. Firstly, we can use books with large pictures of the type discussed just now. Children need to be able to see the pictures from a fair distance; therefore, the colours and the design should be sharp and clear and the detail in the picture kept to a minimum.

Immediate impact is what is required. But remember that pictures are not the be all and end all of stories: they are merely *aids* or reinforcements to the story, though if a child returns to the book on his own later, he may be able to follow the gist of the narrative from the picture sequences.

Secondly, for story books that have more text and fewer pictures, *The Three Billy Goats Gruff* for example, certain aids can be useful. The flannelgraph, whereby a story is read and built up piece by piece and figure by figure, helps children to visualise what the story is about. Large pictures, especially drawn to illustrate the story, are also helpful, though I prefer the flannelgraph because of its flexibility. Children can actually see the story 'growing' in front of them. And, indeed, they can even manipulate the story figures for themselves, creating new events for the story people to do.

Sounds can be a 'back-up' to storytelling. Jean Strachan's *The Bridesmaid*, for example, can be supported by playing a recording of wedding bells and organ music. I have found that this works very well, particularly when a child is going to take part in a wedding as page or bridesmaid.

A final hint for group storytelling is to have children sitting in a circle where they can see and be seen. There is something magical about the circle and there is also something compelling about seeing a person's eyes. So do make sure that every child can both see and hear easily. Moreover, do tell the story slowly. Very young children sometimes have difficulty in catching all the subtle changes of inflexion in our voices and therefore an adult's speech should be slow, clear and distinct. Gestures, if they are not too theatrical, reinforce the characterisation in the story just as a change of voice helps to convey the effect of different people talking. For a story like 'The Three Bears', all you need to do is to pitch the voice high for little bear and low for big bear. This helps tremendously.

Conclusion

In these days of television with its excellent programmes for the younger viewer, it might seem strange that children still find listening to stories attractive. Perhaps the attraction is due to the fascination of the live storyteller whose face and gestures will often communicate as much as the words being spoken, a fascination that preserves something from ancient times when a tribe or village community gathered round the fire and listened to the teller of tales relating myth, parable and fact. Together they shared the wonder and excitement as they listened to the voice. And then talk would follow, only to end as the flames of the fire flickered and died to bring sleep upon all the listeners. A book can have the same effect. It can be a stimulant to the imagination and the intellect; it can be a lullaby and source of conversation; it is always full of profit and delight.

Books for children

The list of books that follows is not in any sense exhaustive but may give some guidance on what books are available and which books have usually been successful with under-fives. Even so, the list is inevitably governed by personal preference and choice. Some books can be used by children after they have been read to them; some can be used only as stories to *tell* since we are dealing almost entirely with pre-reading children. And some books,

Reading together.

especially those of the information type, can be consulted by children themselves but will also be useful as 'talking points'. I have tried to keep to my somewhat arbitrary categories merely to help in the choice of a book for a particular purpose. Obviously there are some books that fit into more than one category or that fit into none! At any rate, the following examples may help you to find your way through the several thousand books for children that now exist.

Myths and fairy tales

Quentin Blake, *Patrick* (Picture Puffin)
        Angelo (Picture Puffin)
Raymond Briggs, *Jim and the Beanstalk* (Picture Puffin)
        Fee Fi Fo Fum (Picture Puffin)
Jean and Laurent De Brunhoff, *Little Babar Books* (Methuen)
Frank Herrmann and George Him, *The Giant Alexander* (Methuen)
Brothers Grimm/Katrin Brandt, *The Elves and the Shoemaker* (Picture Puffin)
Judith Keir, *The Tiger who came to Tea* (Collins Picture Lions)
Gerald McDermott, *Anansi the Spider* (Hamish Hamilton)
Sekiya Miyoshi, *When the World Began* (Methuen)
Helen Nicoll, *Meg on the Moon* (Heinemann)
Sergei Prokofiev, *The Story of Peter and the Wolf* (Faber)
Maurice Sendak, *Where the Wild Things Are* (Picture Puffin)
William Stobbs, *The Story of the Three Bears* (Picture Puffin)
        The Story of the Three Little Pigs (Picture Puffin)

Parabolic stories or fables with a moral

Jean and Gareth Adamson, *Topsy and Tim's Monday Book* (Blackie)
        Topsy and Tim's Thursday Book (Blackie)
        and all the other 'Day' books.
Ruth Ainsworth, *Lucky Dip* (Puffin)
Trude Alberti, *The Animals' Lullaby* (Picture Puffin)
'Althea', *The Gingerbread Band* (Dinosaur Publications)
        Desmond the Dinosaur (Dinosaur Publications)

Leila Berg, The *Nipper* series, especially *Hospital Day* (Macmillan)
Dick Bruna, *Pussy Nell* (Methuen)
　　　　　The *Miffy* books (Methuen)
　　　　　The Christmas Story (Methuen)
Helen Cresswell, *A House for Jones* (Benn)
Dorothy Edwards, *Listen with Mother* (BBC Publications)
　　　　　My Naughty Little Sister (Puffin)
Elve Fortis de Hieronymis, *All the Day Long* (Methuen)
Shirley Hughes, *Lucy and Tom Go to School* (Gollancz)
Pat Hutchings, *Rosie's Walk* (Picture Puffin)
　　　　　Goodnight Owl (Picture Puffin)
Robin and Inge Hyman, *Runaway James and the Night Owl* (Evans)
'Janosch', *Time for Bed* (Dobson)
Ezra Jack Keats, *Peter's Chair* (Picture Puffin)
Claude Laydu, *Freddie Bear's Holiday* (Hamlyn)
Celestino Piatti, *The Happy Owls* (Benn)
D. Ross, *The Little Red Engine gets a Name* (Faber)
Phyllis Rowland, *It is Night* (Bodley Head)
Dr. Seuss, *The Five Hundred Hats of Bartholomew Cubbins* (Collins)
Gene Zion, *Harry the Dirty Dog* (Picture Puffin)

Stories of everyday life

Leila Berg, *The Little Pete Stories* (Puffin)
Eric Carle, *The Very Hungry Caterpillar* (Picture Puffin)
Mary Cockett, *Mary Ann Goes to Hospital* (Methuen)
Michael and Joanne Cole, *Kate and Sam* series (Methuen)
William Cole and Tomi Ungerer, *Frances the Face-maker* (Methuen)
Dorothy Edwards, *Tales of Joe and Timothy* (Methuen)
Adelaide Holl, *The Rainpuddle* (Picture Puffin)
Pat Hutchins, *Changes, Changes* (Picture Puffin)
Ezra Jack Keats, *The Snowy Day* (Picture Puffin)
Pre-school Playgroups Association, *Let's Go Shopping* (Nelson Young World Productions)
Anne and Harlow Rockwell, *The Toolbox* (Picture Puffin)
Jean Strachan, *The Bridesmaid* (Storychair)
　　　　　The Jumble Sale (Storychair)
Gunilla Wolde, *Thomas has a Bath* (Brockhampton Press)

Information books

Ruth Ainsworth and Ronald Ridout, *A book for me to read* series, e.g. *What can you hear?, Susan's House, Colours, What are they?* (Purnell Bancroft)

Josette Blanco, *On the Farm, Sport, The Weather, Playtime* (Child's Play International)

Alain Gree, *Look Around* books, e.g. *Look What Smokes, Look What Goes Round* (Methuen)

Dean Hay, *Now I Can Count* (Collins)

Talkabout Leaders, e.g. *Home, Animals, Water* (Ladybird)

Starters series, e.g. *Sleep, Snow, Cars, Farms, Birds* (Macdonald)

Zero Books for Fun and Learning, e.g. *In the Jungle, At the Circus, In the Zoo, On the Beach, In the Air* (Macdonald)

Pamela Nash, *See how it grows* series, e.g. *The Butterfly, The Seed* (Macmillan)

Beverley Randall and Jill McDonald, *Heavier and Heavier, Less and Less, Further and Further, Fewer and Fewer* (Methuen)

Hilda Smith, *Colourwise* (Macmillan)

Denis Wrigley, *Sand, Size, etc.* (Lutterworth)

Poetry

Come Follow Me (Evans)

Leila Berg, *Four Feet and Two* (Penguin)

Edward Lear, *The Owl and the Pussycat* (Collins Picture Lions)
The Quangle Wangle's Hat (Picture Puffin)

Elizabeth Matterson, *This Little Puffin* (Puffin)

Spike Milligan, *Silly Verse for Kids* (Puffin)

Iona and Peter Opie, *The Oxford Nursery Rhyme Book* (Oxford University Press)

Books for reading beginners

Terry Hall, *Laugh and Learn* series, Books 1 to 6 (Tom Stacey Ltd.)

Helen Piers, *Mouse Looks for a House* (Methuen)
Hullabaloo for Owl (Methuen)

13 Morals, manners and moods

Sooner or later we all discover that some*one* or some*thing* is
in our way. As children grow up, ideally they learn how to cope
with the opposition presented by other people whose rights and
opinions they come to recognise are equal to their own. The
process of learning and coping begins when a child becomes
physically, intellectually and emotionally mobile, and it continues
throughout his life. I find the hardest thing I ever have to do in
life is admit the right of other people to hold opinions different
from mine. But that is what life is all about, at least, the kind of
life in society for which we are or ought to be preparing our
children. A great deal of this preparation can be done if we
appreciate the necessity for morals and manners ourselves and if
we also appreciate the reasons why children behave as they do to
other children, to parents and to teachers.

Perhaps we may discover that anti-social behaviour is the
result of children's moods, for which there are always reasons,
though these may be obscure and not appreciated, or if they are
recognised, frequently ignored by parents and teachers. In any
event, I hope that much of what has been said throughout the
earlier chapters will give some sort of clue to understanding the

behaviour of children in their early years. In this chapter, I want to look particularly at the way in which children's exploration of experience has to be modified by the needs of society. In short, how do children integrate with society and what place do manners and morals play in this process of integration? And how do children's moods affect their behaviour, which to us may often seem anti-social?

The need for morals and manners

Most children are either 'nice' or 'naughty' in the eyes of parents and teachers, and the difference between what we consider being nice and being naughty is usually determined by whether children do what we tell them or not. Unfortunately, children often get a bad name when they do not really deserve it. A family is marked for some inadequacy and the children from the family are accused of suspect behaviour quite unjustifiably. It may be true that we all live up to what society expects of us. If parents or teachers expect us 'to go far', there are fearful repercussions when examinations are failed or we are thrown out of a job. On the other hand, if a teacher expects us to steal the milk money, then we may very well do so. The main cause of this is our own failure to let children and other people be what they are in themselves. Somehow, we have to develop our own personalities in an intensely individual way and at the same time learn how to respect and live in society with others whose temperaments and personalities may be very different from our own. Manners can help us to do this, as I hope we shall see.

In these so-called permissive days, neither morality nor manners are particularly fashionable topics. 'Doing your own thing' has become a worn and wearing phrase which is applied to art in particular and life in general, and ostensibly justifies any self-expressive activity regardless of its aesthetic value or its effect on anyone else. Self-expression is vitally important to us all and especially to young children. But when the only criterion for 'doing your own thing', whether in painting, music, writing or life itself, is that it must be *felt*, any expression of feeling can degenerate into mere self-indulgence and the chance to have an emotional orgy. In short, if children are not 'corrected' at some point—and there are some parents and teachers who would advocate just the opposite—then society is in for a hard time.

However, we are not concerned here with the pros and cons of any philosophy of art, but with the implications morality and manners have for society and some of the ways in which their manners can be encouraged in the home, playgroup and first school.

Morality

Morality is basically concerned with what a society considers to be right and wrong. Every society has its own particular version of morality expressed in rules and laws which its members have found necessary if daily life is to be lived in an orderly way, for without some sort of order based on principles that other members of that society also accept, life could not go on as we know it.

Without rules a game cannot continue and it is the same with life. All rules are, in effect, a means of showing our respect for social structures and the rights of individuals expressed in law and order. In other words, the rules of the game not only protect society from its own self-destruction, but also imply that other people and their opinions are as significant as we imagine ours to be. Particular moral attitudes may change, but morality is a characteristic of human society and prevents it from falling into sheer anarchy. Lack of respect for international law underlies hi-jacking and the taking of hostages to gain some political end, and it is, perhaps, one of the most frightening features of our age. Maybe there is something we can do for our children to help them accept the rules of the game, namely, to learn to live with those whose opinions are violently opposed to their own.

To illustrate what I mean by rules for the very young, we can refer back to earlier chapters in which we discussed the way a child becomes disturbed and anxious when his normal pattern of life is altered. Moving house, or having a different teacher who has a different method of doing things, can cause anxiety expressed in temporary aggression. And, of course, the immigrant child, who has been used to discipline in his home, often finds it almost intolerable to cope with the open-plan school and free movement within it. He just does not understand the rules of that particular game. Because rules and routine are designed to create and maintain a secure and ordered society whether in the home, playgroup or school, they may be a child's first taste of what morality means. But rules can only work if there is mutual respect between all those who belong to that society and everyone needs tolerance and understanding to make the rules effective. In other words, we have to value the rights, beliefs and opinions of every member of the community, whether we agree with them or not. And they must value ours.

Morals, then, are concerned with values, that is to say, with the mutual acceptance of some personal acts and the rejection of others depending on the way they are likely to affect the order and organisation of society. We express this attitude towards values quite simply in terms of 'right' and 'wrong'. And it seems to me that some appreciation of values, particularly that placed on the rights of individuals, should be an essential part of every home and educational system.

Children's attitudes towards morality

Curiously enough, despite what some educators claim, children are usually highly moral. By this I mean that they have a strong sense of justice and fair play. Some of these attitudes may be learnt in the home, but there does seem to be an inherent feeling for order and security in life. And as we have seen, one of the primary functions of fantasy play in whatever form it appears is to attempt to restore order and meaning to the chaos of the actual world. But security depends upon routine, and routine, ritual or repetition, whatever we like to call it, rests on rules. The most secure life for a child is expressed in routine and ritual and children seem to have an obsessive compulsion to keep these rules and maintain this routine. They are very quick to point out to adults that someone is breaking the rules. 'That's not fair!' is the common accusation of the young—and old! But the under-five may have little idea of what 'fairness' means. What upsets him is change in the pattern of his life.

For the very young child, then, morality in terms of an absolute set of values is possibly beyond his comprehension. What he experiences in home and school are rules which regulate his life and give him a sense of security. The routine and rules— the morality, in fact—of his home, playgroup or school are factors partly determined by society itself and partly by parents and teachers. The ideal society for us all would be one in which an individual freely accepted the rules because he knew he was made secure by them. Every game needs a referee whose decisions are final, and every society needs its focus of moral principles, of rules and routine, for survival. In the home, this focus is usually the parents; in school, the teachers. Whatever may be said about 'doing your own thing' and however much we may believe in the importance of self-expression, most of us need to know whether our actions have the approval or disapproval of other people.

When parents say: 'Don't be naughty!' they may not realise that the notion of 'naughtiness' has little or no meaning for a child, apart from the sign of disapproval on his mother's face. She smiles if, in her opinion, he has done 'right' and scowls if he has done 'wrong'. In this very simple sense, a child begins to see 'morality' in his mother's face, or in the response of whoever else he may turn to for approval. Hence, the moral values of adults are extremely important, because they will usually be reflected in the behaviour and attitudes of children. But in these early years a child has not learnt to distinguish sharply between himself and those things which have an existence apart from himself. Being still in the egocentric stage of development we discussed in Chapter 1, he is only beginning to discover his 'territory' and his rights of ownership, that is to say, what is his and what is not.

A common moral problem

Because of this state of affairs in his development, he may not be aware of the difference between living and non-living things. For example, a two-year-old crushes a matchbox. Later, he crushes his brother's pet gerbil and kills it. Is he being deliberately cruel or just careless or what?

One thing is certain: we cannot label him as being 'naughty'. But incidents of this kind, whether in the home or school, raise agonising problems for parents, the rest of the family and for teachers. Two points might help us deal with these difficult situations.

Firstly, we should remember that a two-year-old is the centre of his world. The gerbil is not someone else's and for the child it does not have an independent life. So he is unaware of what belongs to whom. He has not yet formed concepts which enable him to think about 'things' without actually seeing and touching them. Hence, he is unable to realise that they can belong to another person.

Secondly, as observers, we need to recognise, even if we are completely out of sympathy with the child for what he has done, that objects, whether living or not, are just *objects* to him. So if you squash paper, you can squash a gerbil. As one four-year-old remarked on seeing her mother put her foot on a fly shortly after hearing of her grandmother's death, 'Is that how granny died?'

That some things you may kill and some you may not is a notion not yet understood. Similarly, that some things like pet mice, budgerigars, and hamsters are alive and that some things like matchboxes, paper bags and boxes—all of which make delightfully satisfying noises when squashed—are not, has yet to be realised. For the child the connection between all these animals and objects is their 'squashiness' or 'non-squashiness'.

The response of adults to such distressing accidents as the killing of a pet should be to give the child another animal as soon as possible. Let him handle it, though always under supervision. Show him how gently you have to hold little creatures and let him stroke it. But to scold him and tell him he is naughty is meaningless. Naughtiness is usually the description of behaviour which deviates from parental attitudes, and these take time to establish and for a child to accept. Moreover, these attitudes, expressed in various rules for the home, must be reasonable and consistent.

To summarise, the response to such distressing incidents in particular and to any misdemeanour in general must be positive rather than negative. As already mentioned, aggression can be channelled into a useful and constructive activity. And this leads us to make a few points about 'correcting' a child.

Problems occur when the child begins, quite literally, to find his feet. It is not particularly rational though perfectly understandable to say 'Stop that!' when the books are being swept off the shelves. Obviously, we have to stop what the child is doing, but how to do it in a meaningful and constructive way is the real question. And I must stress that there are no easy short cuts to good behaviour. The first thing to do is to see exactly what it is we want children to do with regard to being 'nice', or, if you prefer, 'moral'.

Basic morality

There are really only two rules in morality which make any kind of sense to me: respect for life and respect for property. Neither

156

is possible for an under-five until he has reached the stage of intellectual development we discussed earlier, when concepts have been formed and he is able to differentiate things and people from himself.

Firstly, respect for the rights of other individuals only begins to have meaning as a child moves out into the world of wider social relationships. At first he is emotionally tied to his parents, then gradually he explores relationships with children of his own age. At this stage he might start to snatch at something another child is holding or poke him with inquisitive fingers. These apparently anti-social actions are expressions of curiosity. Naturally, we cannot allow vicious poking and pulling, but we can help to satisfy in a more gentle way the need to explore the existence of another human being.

As Joan Cass points out, social play, that is play in the presence of other children, has been classified under five main headings: 'solitary play, spectator play (when children are concerned in watching each other), parallel play when they like to be near each other, associative play when they often *appear* to be playing together, and genuine co-operative play'. The ages at which each of these stages is reached will obviously depend on the temperament of the child and on the opportunities for easy contact between parents and child, in terms of conversation and doing things together that the home provides.

But until a child is emotionally ready for true co-operative play, in which respect for others is vitally important, there is little point in telling him he is naughty to poke his little brother in the tummy or to take an exploratory tug at his sister's hair. If such things happen—and they certainly will—always try to offer a diversionary course of action for the child to follow: something which is positive, like giving the child who accidentally killed the pet gerbil another animal to hold as soon as possible.

Ultimately, however, respect for the rights of others and acceptance that they have a life of their own depends on the way we treat children in the first place. If we respect *them*, then they will very likely learn to respect *us* and others more easily. But adults do not always treat children with the respect they want their children to give them. For example, talking about a child as if he were not there; clearing up his toys without due warning; destroying his paintings and throwing away his precious 'treasures'; interrupting his conversation and his play: all these acts are frequently done by adults and they will merely create the anti-social behaviour which we condemn in children. Morality begins at home!

Secondly, respect for property can be encouraged in a similar way when children are aware that some things they own and some they do not. At first, an under-five, especially up to the age of two or so, will clutch his possessions, and hold on to them grimly. It seems likely that a possession is a symbol of self-assertion, a natural instinct in all of us, but particularly strong in the very young child who is experimenting with the developing power of his personality. So he may find it difficult to share, to take turns at using a toy in a playgroup and so on.

It is important that a child should become aware that other children's treasures and toys are just as precious as his own. Again, this attitude is best encouraged in the home where a child's own possessions are respected by parents. Perhaps it seems as if I am stressing the function of the parents in giving moral leadership by teaching respect for other people's lives and property, but I have no doubt that this is where it all begins. A mother once complained to me about her five-year-old: 'He's full of fight,' she said, expecting me, as the teacher, to do something about it. But the cause of his aggression lay in the home for reasons which were somewhat obscure. Again, I would emphasise that morality begins at home!

Manners

Whereas morals are essential for social survival, manners, at least superficially, are not. Just as no game could continue without rules, no society could survive for long without the rule of law which is based on morality. Society could exist without manners—for a time—but not without morals.

As we have already discussed, morality is based on respect for others, and respect implies trust. Without respect and trust for other people no relationships can be established between us and them. Simple matters—like telling children the truth, for example —create trust. Children are usually sincere and direct in their dealings with everybody, and young children expect the same treatment from adults as they deal out themselves. It is true that their directness has to be modified by diplomacy or manners in order to prevent people being unnecessarily hurt. But children are quick to see through the deceit of grown-ups. If a child discovers that a parent or teacher has told a lie, it can be the beginning of mistrust, lack of respect and an eventual breakdown in family or class relationships. It can be as simple as that. And many families will know all about this kind of situation.

Usually, the ultimate breakdown in relationships is the result of the slow accumulation of incidents of deceit, dishonesty and insincereity. Herbert Butterfield, a famous contemporary historian, claims that the great catastrophes of history, like the two world wars, are caused by the breakdown of personal relationships and not by tremendously important political decisions, 'A civilisation may be wrecked without any spectacular crimes or criminals but by constant petty breaches of faith and minor complicities on the part of men generally considered very nice people.' If he is right, then our own personal relationships with each other and particularly our relationships with children in our families, playgroups and schools become of supreme importance.

It is one of the functions of manners to modify our brashness, to temper what may be the hurtful truth with tolerance, sympathy and understanding. Manners can prevent us from needlessly offending someone because we have not tried to understand his or her point of view. In practice, we can look at the process of modification in two areas; speech and customs.

Manners and speech

Since manners open up for us the possibility of making social contacts, one of the most important keys to these contacts is speech, for the way we talk to people may pave the way to co-operation and friendship with them. Manners in general may reflect the moral principles based on respect for others, but verbal manners in particular can prevent us from needlessly offending each other. Children should begin to learn the speech forms associated with manners as soon as they can talk, for it is an essential part of our social structure.

Speech and language were discussed at length in Chapter 4, which dealt with language play, but here it is worth emphasising several points relating to manners. For example, in order not to provoke the antagonism of someone we do not know very well, it is necessary to use those speech conventions appropriate to the situation we are in. So our conventional greetings like 'How do you do?' and so on may or may not be genuine enquiries about someone's health and welfare, but are more likely to be a means of exploring the situation to see whether the relationship can be extended. The foundation of friendships, business deals, diplomatic treaties can depend on the formal exchanges of greetings and so on.

Part of the social training in schools is concerned with teaching children to recognise different situations and when you can say one thing and when another: when 'Hi!' might be appropriate and when it might offend. You may remember that we discussed these points in more detail in the chapter on language play, but we can now see, perhaps, that the whole question of speech and language is closely bound up with social conventions and with manners.

When teaching in West Africa I quickly learnt that, despite the reputation for formality that English people have, their manner of greeting and making social contacts appeared almost slap-happy to Africans and inadvertently offended them. African ways of greeting take a whole range of forms, and cover many different social situations. There was one little song that five-year-olds used to sing, partly to help them learn English and partly to introduce them to the more formal aspects of English greetings. The words of the song went something like this: 'How do you do? I'm very pleased to see you. How do you do? I'm very well today.' Stiff and formal maybe, but the children enjoyed singing it and the patterns of our greetings were being established. It is in fact, quite a useful little rhyme for under-fives in this country, who need to learn some of the simple phrases involved in our speech conventions.

Manners and social customs

Shaking hands, using certain gestures of face and hands and body are all signals we learn to interpret as reinforcements of what we say, or expressions of what we think but do not speak.

Under-fives, then, should not only know how and when to say 'Please' and 'Thank you', but how to behave without grabbing the milk and biscuits. Simple conventions prevent accidents which can happen through grabbing and snatching.

There are certain things that do have to be taught if manners are to mean anything. Bad manners are anti-social, even in small ways, like grabbing at someone else's food, and the answer, like so many answers I have given before, is to be as positive as possible. Stop the anti-social act, but immediately divert the child's energy into constructive channels. 'Sit still!', 'Sit up!', 'Don't mess with your food!' and many other commands are all necessary to parents, but leaving it at that is purely negative. Why sit still, sit up and why not squash the spoon in the gravy and potato—it makes a lovely noise, at least to the child! Rather divert the energy of squashing into something constructive— 'Let's try it this way!'

A few final practical points. Make sure that you do not describe children as 'nice' only if they do what you want them to do without questions asked. And do be consistent. If you ask a child to shut the door because of the draught, do not go out yourself a moment after and leave it open! On the other hand, make sure that you do not describe children as naughty, nasty and ill-mannered when they are just asking too many questions and being a bit of a nuisance.

And lastly, there is the problem of dual attitudes towards manners. Just as children have at least two speech forms, one for the home and for school, so they will almost certainly have different social customs and codes of behaviour. Manners, as we have seen, depend on certain values which are not by any means the same in a playgroup or a school as they are at home. The problem, though real enough, is not perhaps as great in practice as it seems to be in theory. Children are mentally very resilient and flexible and are able to pick up the ethos of the community without much difficulty, or, putting the matter another way, they seem to slip into the conventions and decode the customs of the particular group they are in quite easily. The real trouble arises when there is open conflict between the conventions of home and school, when, for example, parents, possibly for political rather than social and educational reasons, urge a child to opt out of the school system which they may claim is 'posh' and 'upper class' or 'middle class'. Again, it seems to me that differences in social customs and codes of behaviour do exist and it would be a horrifyingly uniform society if this were not so. The purpose of discovering manners is to make children sensitive to the *differences* in people's personalities, temperaments, customs and social backgrounds. This, as I have emphasised throughout this chapter, is what morality based on mutual respect is all about.

And manners, the social conventions of speech and codes of behaviour, can help us all to appreciate the *differences* as well as the *similarities* that exist among people.

Quite often, however, children's apparent anti-social behaviour is due not to any innate wickedness but to moods over which under-fives have little control.

Moods

Most of the anti-social acts we have referred to like grabbing, kicking and biting are all acts of aggression and obviously anti-social by any standards. But what causes the aggression? In certain circumstances, we actually tell children to be aggressors. Not in so many words of course, but when we stress the will to win at games, to succeed in some academic examination, or just to do better than anyone else in a vague, unspecified way, we encourage aggression, whether we realise it or not. This is, perhaps unfortunately, an aspect of our competitive society. Self-assertion and fear are probably the only two emotions a child experiences at the moment of birth; assertion to survive and fear to protect himself from danger. We cannot suppress self-assertion or deny its outlet in some form of aggression. It may be that, when aggression is not properly channelled or when it has no reasonable outlet at all, matters get out of hand and individuals find more primitive, irrational and non-human ways of being aggressive.

Our society runs on channelled aggression—up to a point. The manners and morals we have been talking about act as brakes on over-aggression so that a balance is achieved between natural, instinctive self-assertion and social demands. Fame might very well be the spur to aggressive achievements, but society is the bridle to hold us back. The function of aggression, then, must be understood if we are to do anything about the frequently puzzling and annoying behaviour of young children.

Some reasons for aggressive behaviour

Aggression in young children can usually be put down to a child's moods and by this I mean that there are valid reasons for a particular aggressive act. For example, simple jealousy of brothers and sisters may be expressed in hitting out against them.

This is perfectly natural because there is always, even in the best regulated families and classrooms, a tendency for one child to feel 'out of it' sometimes. Favouritism is often hard to avoid but we should try not to show it. Try to compensate the child who is a natural 'loner' by giving him a little more attention than usual. This will help him feel assured of affection.

We have already mentioned the arrival of a new baby in the family which may cause the older child to act aggressively towards toys or other objects. Technically, this process is known as 'displacement activity' and is a common behaviour feature of all animals and humans. Human beings, however, have a wide variety of displacement activities whereas animals are restricted to a few that are typical of their species. As Desmond Morris points out: 'We make use of virtually any trivial actions as outlets for our pent-up feelings. In an agitated state of conflict we may rearrange ornaments, light a cigarette, clean spectacles, glance at a wrist-watch, pour a drink, or nibble a piece of food . . . They occur with particularly high frequency during the initial stages of social encounters, where hidden fears and aggressions are lurking just below the surface.' So a child's aggression may not only be expressed in displaced or transferred aggressive acts, but also in the kind of unnecessary non-functional activities Desmond Morris describes.

Obviously we never condone aggressive behaviour in children, but however angry *you* may be, try not to lose your temper with the child. As quietly as possible, tell him how displeased you are, but do it firmly and with real conviction.

In a playgroup situation a previously quiet child may suddenly have tantrums and apparently take delight in destroying the games and toys of other children. Often, this is caused by some upset at home. Perhaps the child's father has gone away for a while, or his mother has had to go into hospital. The child probably feels that he has been let down and deserted by the very people on whom he has always depended. It is difficult to explain the reasons to a three- or four-year-old to whom reason is not intellectually possible. Again, assurance can help, though it cannot cure. More effective help can be given by telling stories in which these events occur, or in encouraging some form of role-play and dressing up so that a child can recreate order in his temporarily chaotic world. Even more important in dealing with the 'hidden fears and aggressions' which Desmond Morris suggests underly every social encounter, are manners which have evolved for the specific purpose of helping us over the initial stages of making new contacts in society. Play, in all its various forms, can be used to explore these manners and children will discover how they operate in different social situations. In the playgroups and first schools, this co-operative social play is fundamental and will be discussed in the next chapter.

Aggression and self-assertion

Aggression, however, may sometimes be explained in simple terms of self-assertion. Stepping out into the world is both exciting and perilous. A child wants to be independent and safe at the same time. Thus he wants his mother and yet he tries to free himself from his dependence on her. This can cause a kind of love/hate relationship and is particularly strong around the age of two or so when a child is becoming physically more mobile. The love/hate, dependence/independence attitude can issue in aggression alternating with utter submission. A child may hit out at his mother, and tell her that he hates her and wants her to go away. A mother is usually and quite understandably upset when a child says things like this, mainly because she does not understand what is happening; that, in fact, he loves her but wants to explore his growing independence of her. Yet he is scared to do so, because the world is big and frightening.

Because he is suddenly scared, he will sometimes revert to being a baby, perhaps pretending to be one in his play, or acting in what we call 'a babyish way'. We might even say to him: 'Don't be a baby!' which of course is precisely what he does want to be at that moment. Try to understand the reasons for his behaviour in this case; be sympathetic and it will pass.

A more serious cause of aggression in these days is seen in children who have had little opportunity for play because of their surroundings. High-rise flats, in particular, prevent much free movement and it is difficult for mother to keep an eye on her child twelve or more storeys below in the play area. But if this area is not used, there is little space to play in elsewhere. In fact, children who lack play areas will often find it quite impossible to express their natural exuberance and emotions in physical play. Hence their feelings explode in aggressive behaviour towards parents, other children and other people's property. Playgroups and education for the under-fives in general are only part of the answer to this very real social problem which is partly of our own making. As one child psychologist said to me: 'Why couldn't we predict what would happen with buildings like this and schools of tremendous numbers?' But these matters were not predicted and the best we can do for this type of anti-social behaviour is to provide play facilities in organised groups. Alternatively, as I shall describe in the following chapter, families might try to co-operate with each other to give their children opportunities for group play.

Aggression in itself is not anti-social and it is to be expected that as the child moves out into the world he will meet people and things which get in his way and oppose him. He cannot master all of them, so he may attempt to destroy what he cannot control or comprehend. Adults, too, frustrate him because they prevent him from doing things that he wants to do, some of which might be dangerous. Again, he does not understand the reasons for grown-ups saying 'No' to him. Be patient, firm, and consistent and he will eventually realise that these are the rules of the game and are necessary to him in giving the security that he desires.

Aggression, hostility and bad temper are very likely due to moods and these must be understood, so that the manners and morals that help us control the moods we too experience may become part of the child's world. We probably all have a primitive instinct to hit someone on the head at some time. Children certainly feel this urge if parental affection is apparently withdrawn for some reason or if their property is not respected. But society decrees that hitting people over the head is not permitted. Hence, we turn to play and in play sequences we are learning how to modify our moods—we are, in fact, playing with morals and manners. The importance of all forms of play in helping children meet the demands of society and express their feelings at the same time is very great indeed. As Joan Cass points out: 'Play is one of the most important ways in which children learn that feelings can be safely expressed, that aggression and hostility can be controlled and managed and that its energy is available to be used constructively'.

14 Playing with others

It is absolutely essential for a child to have various opportunities to experiment with the increasing independence he feels. He can do this by seeking new relationships with other children who are not members of his immediate family. A failure by parents to recognise this need and consequently a failure to provide such opportunities can cause a serious restriction of a child's emotional development and thus affect his ability to cope with the new situations and the new people he will have to meet later in life, especially when he starts first school.

Some parents over-protect their children, because it gives their ego a subconscious boost if they feel that they are totally indispensable. Sometimes a mother may say that her four-year-old will certainly not be happy if he is left alone to play with friends either at a party or at a playgroup. Usually she is deceiving herself in this respect. The one thing her child probably wants more than anything else, at least for his own personal development, is to be alone for a while so that he can explore those new avenues of experience in the various ways we have been describing throughout this book, particularly in the company of other children.

Playing together.

The protection racket operates in the parent/child relationship quite openly, and unfortunately, those parents who believe that they are doing the very best for their children in protecting them from life's challenges are possibly doing the very opposite. So, not only for the child's benefit but also for parents', the play-group movement, especially where there is parent involvement in the work, is invaluable. But before saying more about play-groups in general, there is another factor working against children's natural exploration of relationships and environment which needs a brief comment.

In these days of high-rise flats and unfenced gardens or no gardens at all, there is very little space in which children can play in safety. Lack of playing space is a serious handicap for children, who need areas where they can experiment with and show off their developing physical powers. For this reason, the value of outings and visits to interesting places, which need be no further than the pond in the park or the local zoo, lies not only in the new experiences presented, but also in the sheer pleasure it gives children who are able to run, jump and shout without constantly having to be told to sit still and be quiet because of the neighbours next door or underneath.

Somehow all these drawbacks must be overcome, since children need each other and they need space, partly to experiment with growing independence and partly to learn how to live without the constant attention and presence of adults. If such co-operative playing with other children can be arranged on an informal basis, the transition from life at home to life at school will be very much easier and more confidently tackled by a child.

A simple solution is obviously for the children of two families to play together for a morning, perhaps each home taking it in turns to act as the 'homeground'.

There is no doubt that if children can be invited freely into the home, so much the better, and if there is a room or a shed in which they can play and 'make a mess', there is little for anyone to worry about. But if these opportunities or facilities cannot be offered in the home, for whatever reasons, they must be provided elsewhere. And this is where the playgroups and nursery schools come into their own.

Playgroups

After much pressure from parents and social workers, it has become official government policy to encourage education for the under-fives. But it will take some time before all the recommendations are implemented on an official basis. In the meantime, playgroups are proliferating all over the country. Some are excellent and geared to a child's needs as we have been outlining them.

Most parents are concerned about the well-being of their children, emotionally, physically and intellectually, so they need some guidance on what playgroups are trying to do, and if there is a choice, guidance on what to look for when deciding to send their children to a playgroup. In the absence of official evaluation of playgroup standards, this guidance seems to me vitally important. Here, then, are just a few pointers for those parents who, for various reasons, are considering sending their children to a playgroup. And I am assuming, of course, that they will be concerned about what happens there and want the best kind of happy, stimulating environment for their under-fives.

168

Administratively, there are two main types of playgroup. The first has a supervisor (often the 'owner' of the group), some paid helpers and no mother involvement. (It is as well to ask about the question of mother involvement when making enquiries or visiting the playgroup for the first time.) There are many excellent playgroups of this kind and the controversy over the value of mother involvement continues to rage. Personally, though I recognise the problems of working mothers, I strongly believe in mother involvement because it implies a broader concept of education. Mother and child are learning together, and, if fathers can be involved too, so much the better! This leads us to the second type of playgroup.

The second type is usually run by a committee of local mothers who employ a paid supervisor and assistant, and who also require mothers to do a certain number of duties each term. The value of this type of organisation is that mothers are learning about children as much as children are learning about each other, and they can observe the way their own children develop in making relationships and gaining confidence. There is usually a strong sense of community amongst mothers involved in this work, and this is clearly reflected in the atmosphere in the group as a whole.

In assessing the quality of what actually goes on in a playgroup, it is essential to understand the meaning of play and its various forms described throughout the preceding chapters. As we have seen, children learn through play, so a main point to look for is what opportunities are provided for children to engage in these various forms of play. This is a general point, but there are more specific ones which we can take note of.

Firstly, is there a happy, relaxed atmosphere with plenty of easy chatter among children, and between children and the supervisor and helpers? A well organised playgroup should not have children sitting permanently at desks or little tables in imitation of an old-fashioned school. Children should be moving freely and confidently about the room with the supervisor suggesting and guiding rather than imposing activities on them.

Do not worry too much about noise level. The experienced supervisor knows what level of noise to tolerate, and if children are happily banging nails or experimenting with musical instruments, 'shakers', bells and so on, look for children's absorption in what they are doing, rather than criticise the noise. If the children are really involved, they will hardly notice the visitor!

Secondly, look out for pieces of large apparatus like climbing frames, wendy houses, hidey-holes and old cardboard boxes. Is there a dressing-up box full of old clothes, hats and shoes? Do the children use these clothes without being told to do so? Try to do a little discreet eavesdropping on the conversation around and inside the wendy house. Conversation develops out of co-operative playing and it will indicate how well children are integrating.

Apart from these individual activities in which children are constantly forming and reforming groups—a friend for a day or a week is common—there ought to be a period when children come together in order to listen to a five-minute story, sing a song or talk about the weather. There may also be a time for marching, or dancing to music with a strong rhythmic beat. Coming together in this way is encouraging a sense of community and is a vital function of the playgroup's work.

Finally, watch for group play activities like preparation for visits to doctors and dentists. And notice the way children are 'handled'. Gentle firmness towards the children, rather than sentimental coddling, should characterise the adults' manner.

The main thing to assess in a playgroup is whether it is a child-centred or parent-centred. By this I mean whether the child's needs for a lifetime or the mother's freedom for a morning are being catered for.

When visiting a playgroup do remember that there are bad mornings as well as good. You may arrive on a day when everything has gone wrong, so one or two visits should be made if possible. If the supervisor is doing her job well, she will be only too pleased to discuss matters with you, but she may prefer to do this later. No one should expect her to devote a whole morning to enquiries when she is busy with thirty children. And the children are the people who really matter in the playgroup.

One final word about nursery schools. Some playgroups describe themselves as 'nursery schools' because it seems to add a touch of prestige to their work. Technically and administratively they are not nursery schools at all. Officially, a nursery school is one administered by a local education authority. It will probably have its own premises and a fully qualified nursery teacher in charge. In the future, with government support, many first schools are likely to have nursery classes attached to their main schools and they will take children in at four years old.

Some first schools do this anyway.

There are many arguments for and against including under-fives in the organisation of local authority first schools. For instance, there may be a tendency on the part of some parents to regard the system as offering just more school a bit earlier. There may or may not be mother involvement—and this will depend largely on local needs and circumstances, but in official nursery schools mothers will probably not be *officially* involved. In the meantime, however, playgroups as distinct from nursery schools are likely to continue well into the foreseeable future. And in any case, the points I mentioned as worth looking for in a playgroup also apply to a nursery school. So, whether your child goes to a playgroup or a nursery school, at least you will have some idea of what is being done there and why.

For information on playgroups in your area, write to:
Pre-school Playgroups Association,
Alford House, Aveline Street, London, SE11,
or 304 Maryhill Road, Glasgow, NW.

15 Conclusion

A child's instinctive urge for survival, expressed in self-assertion and fear—assertion to master his environment and fear to give him caution—provides him with the initial impetus to explore the unknown. But the steps he takes into this brand-new world can become shorter and less certain unless we do some prodding and propping, in other words, unless we stimulate him in various ways on the one hand, and give him security, love and affection on the other.

Throughout this book I have tried to show how play has many facets, all of which are necessary if a child is to achieve a full and independent life. Playing by oneself eventually develops towards playing with others, and in this way, everyone of us learns to live in society with varying degrees of success. Much of that success depends to a large extent on the kind and quality of play opportunities we have been given.

But without stimuli the impetus towards exploration may die. So tools and toys, books and music, people and places, talking and making should be part and parcel of every child's experience.

Unfortunately, parents who did not have a childhood filled with the opportunities to play sometimes find it difficult to understand their own child's need for them. Parents who for one reason or another have not experienced the love and care of mother and father in a secure and happy family relationship may not find it easy to give that love and care to their own children. Or rather, though they may truly love their children and care for them deeply, they may not quite know how to express their affection. If their own parents fought shy of the physical expression of this love and concern, they may turn away from it themselves. Consequently, there will be a lack of physical and possibly emotional contact between parent and child and between child and the outside world.

Indeed, some parents may even regard the emotions as somewhat frightening, either because they have never learnt to deal with them adequately themselves or because they have failed to understand their function. Hence they may try to suppress a child's emotions. 'Don't cry!', 'Don't be a baby!' and 'Be a man!' they say. Yet emotions properly channelled and controlled are vital to a balanced life. Aggression and fear, for example, are necessary for physical survival whilst grief and joy are essential to our mental health. If we forget how to cry, we may soon forget how to laugh, and laughter and tears are safety valves through which our anguish and tensions are released. Children, too, need emotional safety valves, though we do have to distinguish between tears and temper!

As I hope I made clear in the first chapter of this book, the physical expression of love can secure a child on a base from which he can make the emotional and intellectual explorations he needs. Having taken his risks in play, he can return to 'base' to recover!

Of course, these explorations should not be hurried. Some children grow up too soon. Sometimes, because they are members of a large family, they learn all too quickly how to fend for themselves before they are emotionally ready to cope. Sometimes a parent pushes a child too hard and too fast intellectually, and though a rising five can read he may have no idea how to control his emotions or even what to do with them. 'He's mad!' we say, unthinkingly. Of course he is 'mad', because you cannot bypass a stage in development. The child has probably not played enough with his emotions and with his physical powers. And he must pass through all these phases in play before he can become a whole person, a fully grown 'personality'.

Do give children time to grow up and let them grow at their

own built-in pace. They cannot be forced like a hothouse plant. everyone needs time to play, time to grow, and a secure and happy atmosphere in which to do it. All animals play, but only human beings have the ability to imagine, to create fantasies and therefore to predict what might be and to evolve new forms, new arts, new technologies. Play is the essence of humanity which makes this possible. Margaret Lowenfeld in her book *Play in Childhood* comments: 'Play is to a child, therefore, work, thought, art and relaxation, and cannot be pressed into any single formula. It expresses a child's relation to himself and his environment, and, without adequate opportunities for play, normal and satisfactory emotional development is not possible'.

Only you as a parent or as a teacher can know whether you are giving the stimuli and the love a child needs and indeed must have. Maybe the sanity and the future of the world will ultimately depend on how seriously we treat the human hunger for play.

References

Chapter 1
The Philosophy of Existentialism, Gabriel Marcel (Citadel Press, New York)

Chapter 2
The Naked Ape, Desmond Morris (Corgi)
An Introduction to Child Drama, Peter Slade (University of London Press)
The Child's Conception of the World, Jean Piaget (Paladin)

Chapter 3
Play, Dreams and Imitation in Childhood, Jean Piaget (Routledge)
The Psychology of Play, Susanna Millar (Penguin)
A Rumour of Angels, Peter Berger (Penguin)
Tree and Leaf, J. R. R. Tolkien (Allen & Unwin)
Where the Wild Things Are, Maurice Sendak (Picture Puffin)
Melanie Klein (Hogarth Press)

Chapter 4
Telltales, Sets 1–4, Denis and Judy Gahagan (Evans)

Chapter 5
The Feast of Fools, Harvey Cox (Harvard University Press)
Four Quartets, T. S. Eliot (Faber)
A Rumour of Angels, Peter Berger (Penguin)
Tree and Leaf, J. R. R. Tolkien (Allen & Unwin)
Where the Wild Things Are, Maurice Sendak (Puffin)
Lucky Dip, Ruth Ainsworth (Puffin)
The Little Pete Stories, Leila Berg (Puffin)

Chapter 6
The Empty Space, Peter Brook (Penguin)
An Introduction to Child Drama, Peter Slade (University of London Press)

Chapter 7
Choosing Toys for Children, Sten Hegeler (Tavistock Publications)
An Introduction to Child Drama, Peter Slade (University of London Press)
The Nursery Years, Susan Isaacs (Routledge)

Chapter 9
The Psychology of Play, Susanna Millar (Pelican)

Chapter 10
Pre-school and Infant Art, Kenneth Jameson (Studio Vista)

Chapter 11
The Lore and Language of Schoolchildren, Peter and Iona Opie (Oxford University Press)
This Little Puffin, Elizabeth Matterson (ed) (Puffin)
Music, Starters series (Macdonald)
What Can You Hear?, Ronald Ridout and Ruth Ainsworth (Bancroft)

Chapter 12
The Significance of Children's Play, Joan Cass (Batsford)

Chapter 13
Christianity and History, Herbert Butterfield (Fontana)
The Naked Ape, Desmond Morris (Corgi)
The Significance of Children's Play, Joan Cass (Batsford)

Chapter 15
Play in Childhood, Margaret Lowenfeld (Portway)

Suggestions for further reading

Children and Stories, Anthony Jones and June Buttrey (Blackwell)
Particularly useful for the teacher who may wish to do some
follow-up work on stories and responses to them. A useful list of
suitable stories for various age ranges is given at the end of the
book.

The Child, the Family and the Outside World, D. W. Winnicott
(Penguin)
A very readable short book which concentrates on the infant
stages of growth and behaviour. Particularly useful for mothers.

The Child's Conception of the World, Jean Piaget (Paladin)
One of the standard works on the growth of a child's mind and his
awareness of the world of thought.

A Child's Mind, Muriel Beadle (University Paperbacks)
A technical account of current thinking in the field of child
development psychology.

The Child's World, Phyllis Hostler (Penguin)
A readable and informed account of various aspects of child development. It deals with such matters as the only child and the necessity for fear.

Choosing Toys for Children, Sten Hegeler (Tavistock Publications)

Class, Codes and Control, Basil Bernstein (Paladin)

Craft : Can I Make Another One?, Dorothy Gilbert (Faber)

Education in the Early Years, ed. Maurice Chazan (University of Swansea)
One of the few attempts to deal with education of the under-fives in a scientific and scholarly way.

Enjoying Books, Geoffrey Trease (Phoenix House)

Exploration and Language, Alice Yardley (Evans)

The Feast of Fools, Harvey Cox (Harvard University Press)
An excellent book dealing with the concept of play and the human need for play.

First Art, Warren Farnworth (Evans)
A book which deals specifically with the practical aspects of art for under-fives, with brief accounts of the philosophy of play underlying it.

The First Five Years of Life, Arnold Gesell (Methuen)
A standard work. The division of a child's development into months and years should be treated with caution.

Focus on Meaning, Joan Tough (Allen & Unwin)

The Foundation of Language, Andrew Wilkinson (Oxford University Press)

Four to Fourteen, Kathleen Lines (Cambridge University Press)
A useful general survey, though mainly concerned with the older child.

Homo Ludens, J. H. Huizinga (Paladin)
A classic work for those who wish to study in depth the anthropology of play.

The Human Zoo, Desmond Morris (Corgi)

An Introduction to Child Drama, Peter Slade (University of London Press)
This book has some very useful comments on the nature of play.

The Lore and Language of Schoolchildren, Peter and Iona Opie (Oxford University Press)
Invaluable for anyone who wishes to explore the origins and meaning of children's singing games and playground rhymes.

Literature and the Young Child, Joan Cass (Longman)
An excellent book which includes a long list of recommended books for the under-fives. The chapter on the fantasy tale is especially recommended.

The Multiracial Class, Paul Widlake (Evans)
Contains some helpful chapters on the language problems of immigrant children.

The Naked Ape, Desmond Morris (Corgi)

Not Yet Five, E. Gwenda Bartram (Geoffrey Hart)
An excellent short book giving advice to mothers on providing play opportunities in the house. Especially useful if no playgroup is available.

The Nursery Years, Susan Isaacs (Routledge)
One of the earliest books in its field. Now a little out of date but still standard reading for those involved with young children. It contains some useful chapters on practical ways of dealing with behaviour problems.

Our Language, Simeon Potter (Pelican)

The Penguin Playgroup Book, Joyce Lucas and Vivienne McKennell (Penguin)
All the practical details about the running of a playgroup with a section on play activities.

Play, Dreams and Imitation in Childhood, Jean Piaget (Routledge)

The Playgroup Book, Marie Winn and Mary Ann Porcher (Fontana)
A guide for mothers who wish to run a playgroup for their children. The book is full of valuable ideas for children's play activities, and contains a particularly informative chapter on music complete with lists of suitable song books and records.

The Playgroup Movement, Brenda Crowe (Playgroups Association)
The standard work on the playgroup movement by the National Adviser to the Pre-school Playgroups Association. It offers an excellent account of the reasons why playgroups are necessary and the various ways in which they are organised.

Play School Play Ideas, Ruth Craft (BBC Publications)
Contains many suggestions for making things from different materials, including junk. Also contains action rhymes which can be used in playgroups. Most of the ideas were first presented on the BBC's 'Playschool' programme.

Play with a Purpose for Under-sevens, Elizabeth Matterson (Penguin)
A very practical book containing particularly useful sections on music and the making of instruments, and ideas for encouraging all forms of art, including junk creations.

Pre-school and Infant Art, Kenneth Jameson (Studio Vista)

The Pre-school Years, Willem van der Eyken (Penguin)
Contains a lucid account of the history of pre-school education and a short but comprehensive survey of the social reasons for advocating education for under-fives.

The Psychology of Play, Susanna Millar (Pelican)
A simply written, comprehensive account of what psychologists have thought and are thinking about the nature of play. It is particularly concerned with fantasy in childhood.

180

The Self-respecting Child, Alison Stallibrass (Thames & Hudson)
Contains detailed accounts of children playing with an analysis of
the spontaneous element in play.

The Significance of Children's Play, Joan Cass (Batsford)
A simple study containing many practical hints on how to encourage children's play and how to deal with hostility and aggression through play. There are chapters on water play, clay,
painting and dressing up.

Spoken English, Andrew Wilkinson (University of Birmingham,
   School of Education)

Talk Reform, Denis and Judy Gahagan (Routledge)

Toys down the Ages, J. Hornby (Chatto & Windus)
A delightfully illustrated book which shows how important the
function of toys has been throughout history. The mechanics
and materials of toys are described, and could provide ideas for
making toys.

Young Children Thinking, Alice Yardley (Evans)
A clear and readable account of the way in which children learn
to think. This is a complementary book to the author's *Exploration and Language*.

Your Five Year Old, Elsie L. Osborne (Corgi)

Your Four Year Old, Elsie L. Osborne (Corgi)

Your One Year Old, Dilys Daws (Corgi)

Your Three Year Old, Dina Rosenbluth (Corgi)

Your Two Year Old, Dina Rosenbluth (Corgi)

Index